Edinburgh After Dark

Ron Halliday

BLACK & WHITE PUBLISHING

First published 2010
by Black & White Publishing Ltd
29 Ocean Drive, Edinburgh EH6 6JL

1 3 5 7 9 10 8 6 4 2   10 11 12 13
ISBN: 978 1 84502 289 1
Copyright © Ron Halliday, 2010

A CIP catalogue record for this book is
available from the British Library.

Typeset by Ellipsis Books Ltd, Glasgow
Printed and bound by MPG Books Ltd, Bodmin

Edinburgh After Dark

Contents

Contents

Acknowledgements

Edinburgh has always fascinated me as a city which, although it maintains a dignified outward appearance, possesses many hidden depths. The paranormal certainly occupies one of them. To those who don't know it, the city may appear almost staid. Those who have experienced it feel differently. It's a hot spot of the weird and wonderful with the supernatural one of its most intriguing aspects. Many examples of the capital's hidden side I have documented in *Edinburgh After Dark*. But, as I have found, no book is an island and its birth is dependent on many things. Having spent almost thirty years investigating the paranormal my thanks first and foremost must go to all those who have been witness to, or have been directly involved in, strange and inexplicable events. Without their willingness to report their experiences this book could not have been written. For personal reasons not all witnesses have wished to have their full names disclosed, and some have asked that a pseudonym be used and I have, of course, respected their wishes. In some very recent cases I have made sure, as requested, that exact locations cannot be identified. I would like to express my thanks to Gary Gray for sharing his psychic experience and knowledge with me and for various insights over the years, to Andrew Hennessey (www.stargateedinburghtours.com), Harry Sommerville, Malcolm Robinson, and Mark Fraser.

I'm grateful to all those writers, from long times past and more recently, whose observations, reports and comments have stimulated my own thoughts and I'd particularly mention recent works by Lorraine Evans and David Miles. Books by the long gone Robert Chambers and James Grant are a mine of information on 'old Edinburgh'. Other sources I have found useful are mentioned in the text. Appreciation to Rab McNeil for allowing me to make use of his article on the 'Hunter's Tryst Haunting' and to Dr R. Halliday, Mr H. Macdonald, and Euan and Jackie for providing me with additional information. I would like to thank members of the 'Scottish Earth Mysteries' group which investigates the paranormal and of which I am Chairman for their support over the years and, in particular, to Brian Wilson for his report on the Niddry Vaults investigation. You can find us on the web at www.ufo-scotland.co.uk or at www.ronhalliday.co.uk

I would like to thank Janne, John and Alison at Black & White Publishing for seeing through the production, and Black & White Publishing for its continuing interest in publishing books on the paranormal. Finally, a big thanks to my wife Evelyn for tolerating my long absences while writing *Edinburgh After Dark*, for suggestions as to what might be included and for reading over (several times!) the text.

Ron Halliday

1

City of Mystery

Is it possible that thousands of years ago an Egyptian princess visited Scotland and made the site where Edinburgh now stands her capital? In September 2009, mystic Uri Geller made a strange claim. He argued that an island in the Firth of Forth, known as 'The Lamb', had links to the ancient Egyptians and that treasure brought to Scotland by an Egyptian Princess called Scota, could be buried there. Whether or not ancient artefacts are hidden on this small island off the coast of North Berwick, Uri Geller brought to public attention a fact long hidden from the Scottish public. Edinburgh may have been founded by the same civilisation that built the pyramids. And Scotland might have been named after the Egyptian princess Scota. Although most historians do not accept the link, the belief has been long held in Scotland and was recorded as fact by writer Walter Bower, in the fifteenth century, in his book *The Chronicles of Scotland.* In recent years, whatever the official view, such ideas have received a boost from work carried out by scientists using the latest DNA technology, which has revealed that there is a significant genetic link between today's inhabitants of Scotland and people of the Near East. That by no means proves that Scotland was colonised by Egyptians and may simply point to migration across Europe thousands of years ago. It is intriguing, nonetheless, especially when other facts are considered.

To add to the mystery there is evidence that the Picts, who at one time were the ruling tribe in Scotland, may have their origin in the land of Scythia, an ancient country bordering the Middle East. Furthermore, traces of Cornish tin in Egyptian-made objects points to the fact that, thousands of years ago, trading was taking place right across the Mediterranean Sea and would surely have included Scotland. There are certainly names across Scotland which suggest an Egyptian influence. There is the River Isis, near Blairgowrie, for one. Isis was, of course, one of the key goddesses in the religion of the Ancient Egyptians. A river bearing her name shows that a cult of Isis was at one time active in the area, and that surely cannot have been an isolated event. Over the years other ancient names, which once existed, have simply been overlaid by newer ones. Some have survived though. The River Nith in Dumfriesshire bears close resemblance to the name of an Egyptian goddess and, interestingly, there was at least one queen of Ancient Egypt called Neith. A pyramid, still standing, marks her burial place.

More proof of a link with Scotland comes in the shape of faience beads, which have been shown to be identical to those found on necklaces from Amarna, the ancient Egyptian city built by the Pharaoh Akhenaten, and dating to 1350 BC. They have been found in several locations across Scotland. In addition a pear-shaped white glass bead discovered near Arbroath was similar to beads from the time of the eighteenth Egyptian dynasty, around three thousand years ago. It is also incredible but true that, in 1937, the remains of three Egyptian boats were discovered beneath centuries of mud in the Humber Estuary at North Ferriby, only a comparatively short journey from the Lothian coast. It is to be wondered what else waits to be discovered about this long-hidden connection. It all suggests that Ancient Egypt and Scotland might well have been known to each other and that the alleged 'myth' of this contact might have some basis in fact.

There is another strange link to the capital. The 'Blue Blanket' has long been a symbol of Edinburgh. Up to the 1970s, a pub called the 'Blue Blanket' stood in the heart of the Royal Mile testifying to its enduring appeal. Blue rather than green was the traditional Scottish symbol of the 'other world', of the mystic realms, as in the 'Blue men of the Minch', the mythical sea creatures who dwelt in the depths of the sea. So where did this tradition come from? The usual account tells us that, in 1482, King James III was being held prisoner in Edinburgh Castle. The citizens of the capital came out to support him and helped free the king. As a gesture of thanks James granted the trades people of the city the right to display a banner, which was to be used when rallying the citizens of Edinburgh to defend the capital. This banner came to be called the 'Blue Blanket'. However, some have cast doubt on this traditional tale suggesting that the banner had, in fact, a far older pedigree and had been taken to the Holy Land during the Crusades. This might suggest that James had given the city a banner which already had an ancient history, and that the banner was already seen as having a mystical association.

But why the name and how did it link to the monarchy? A clue may be found in the Berlin Museum. Displayed there is an inscribed stone, called a 'stela', on which is carved the figures of two rulers, one of whom is wearing what is known as the 'Blue crown'. One of the carvings has been identified as Akenhaten and the other as his wife Nefertiti. It was their daughter, the legendary Scota, who allegedly came to Scotland. So did Scota bring the belief in the mystical significance of the colour blue to Edinburgh? It's a tantalising thought and there's

no doubt that much remains to be unearthed about our connection with the ancient Egyptians.

Indeed other aspects of the city are connected to the ancient
world if the writer Comyns Beaumont is to be believed.
According to Beaumont, who wrote two detailed books on the
subject, archaeologists have misunderstood ancient history. He
argued — after extensive research of ancient biblical texts,
Greek writings and Pictish carved stones among others — that
the ancient Greeks and Phoenicians lived not in the
Mediterranean, but in Scotland. Mount Olympus was not
located in Greece, but was actually Ben Nevis.

His ideas might seem hard to swallow, but recent evidence
has emerged which may provide some support for his theories.
Research by linguistic experts has identified a lost language of
Scotland. It appears that in addition to Pictish and Gaelic there
existed, thousands of years ago, a third language, few traces of
which remain. But it was a language which experts believe was
similar to that spoken in Phoenicia, the ancient biblical land
occupying the area where modern-day Israel and the Lebanon
now stand. This discovery did not emerge till many years after
Beaumont published his work in the 1940s. In Beaumont's
mind, Edinburgh occupied pride of place. It was, in fact, the
true Jerusalem as described in the Bible; the very place where
Jesus walked and was crucified. He identified Arthur's Seat as
the actual Mount of Olives, the hill so strongly linked in the
Bible to the last year of Jesus' mission. The biblical 'City of
Zion' was, in his view, a fortress on the rock where Edinburgh
Castle now stands, and 'Joppa' was the actual port of the same
name recorded in the Old Testament. According to Beaumont,
a natural catastrophe only a few thousand years ago, a comet
strike he suggested, had forced the 'Greeks' and 'Phoenicians'
to flee from Scotland and settle in the Mediterranean. So
Jerusalem, which had really been Edinburgh, became linked

4

*Arthur's Seat – the mystic heart of Edinburgh where
strange miniature coffins were hidden underground, maybe
to cast a Satanic spell.*

instead to the biblical land of Israel. Whatever the reality, Beaumont's ideas are a testament to the hold that the 'magic' of Edinburgh can have on an individual's imagination.

Beaumont seemed unaware of it, but there was an ancient tradition that connected Edinburgh and Jerusalem. Legend claimed that the capital's 'City Guard', a group which patrolled the 'Old Town' and maintained law and order, were present in Jerusalem at the time Jesus was crucified. At that time they took from the Temple an original portrait of King Solomon for safekeeping. The painting, if it ever existed, is long gone and we need not take this story at face value, but it does suggest that there was a belief that the Holy Land and Scotland's capital city were bound by a special relationship. And that need

5

not appear as fanciful as it seems. Recent investigation by Edinburgh's Gordon Strachan, detailed in *Jesus the Master Builder,* has suggested that Jesus may have visited Scotland and discussed religious matters with the Druids. There is even a tradition that Jesus was born in Scotland and was taken to the 'Holy Land' as a child. Whatever the truth, it suggests a hidden link connecting Scotland to biblical events with which it was long believed we had no involvement.

But how is it that the site where Edinburgh now stands has always been seen as a place of such importance? Was there a special aura that our ancestors associated with this part of Scotland, located between the Pentland Hills and the Firth of Forth? A clue may be found in Rosslyn Chapel. On its own Rosslyn Chapel has earned a reputation that ranks it as one of the world's key mystery sites. But enigmatic as it is, I would argue that it is but one part of a wider mystery that takes in a range of strange locations stretching right across the city, and which, in addition, form an interlocking puzzle. However, we will take Rosslyn Chapel as a starting point. The strange figures which adorn the ceiling and pillars and its links to both the Knights Templar and Freemasons have encouraged wide speculation, but little has been said about a number of lesser-known aspects of the chapel. For centuries before the building was erected the area was known as a place where strange lights and objects appeared. As early as the sixth century AD, the mystic and religious leader St Mungo visited the area and, indeed, a well named after him, which was believed to cure the sick, existed in nearby Penicuik. Mungo, who later became the patron saint of Glasgow, was a man who was believed to posses supernatural powers and although he is now linked more to Scotland's west coast he was in fact the son of a Lothian princess who miraculously survived attempts to drown her in the Firth of Forth. Mungo's visits to Rosslyn show that long before the chapel existed this location was seen as having some type of mystical attraction.

Furthermore, can it just be coincidence that Rosslyn Chapel was built within sight of the Pentland Hills? It has always struck me as odd, however, that though several writers have discussed the mysteries of the chapel no one has considered previously the strange aura that exists around the Pentlands. I would go as far as to suggest that Edinburgh and sites such as Rosslyn Chapel were chosen because of their proximity to these hills. In my view, they are the most sacred of the locations in this area. There is some support for this from the very word 'Pentland' which, according to Peter Drummond's *Scottish Hill Names,* was coined during the twelfth century to describe the hills. It may actually be an amalgamation of the words 'pen' and 'llan' meaning the heights above enclosed land and a church. From early times, it seems, the Pentland Hills and the future site of Rosslyn Chapel were closely linked.

The Pentlands, which form an imposing backdrop, both spiritually and physically, to the capital, have been the source of many strange events for centuries, including bizarre balls of light which move and hover and seem to be driven by some weird intelligence. Such lights continue to appear. In the Autumn of 1989, at High Camilty, a shining white light was seen hovering over a field close to an isolated house. It had first been observed travelling down the slopes of the Pentlands at speed, but stopped for several minutes as if deciding where to go next. It then moved towards the house at about tree height and came within two hundred yards of the bedroom window, where the family stood watching, before it halted then slowly retreated. But this was by no means an isolated incident and strange lights, moving both slowly and rapidly, have been reported in this area on many occasions.

But do the Pentland Hills hold an even stranger secret which explains why our ancestors found this area such a spiritual heartland? It's an incredible fact that the outline of the Pentland Hills, when viewed from certain areas with the sun behind them, form the shape of an enormous goddess figure. The best time to witness this strange phenomenon is during the period of the winter solstice in December. It has been suggested that the hills were deliberately modified to achieve this effect, but it may be no more than simply the chance of nature. Such a phenomenon is rare, but has been noted at other spots in Scotland. The Isle of Skye springs to mind. And the mysterious shape formed by the Pentland Hills might fit well with the idea of the *Cailleach*, the ancient Celtic goddess of winter who represents cold, darkness and death. The *Cailleach*, according to legend, turns to rock when summer comes and the possibility that the Pentland Hills were seen as representing the *Cailleach* is tantalising. When Christianity arrived the *Cailleach* was transformed into St Bridget, the protector of the harvest, and the polar opposite of the pagan Pentland goddess.

The capital has, as might be guessed, been host to a number of strange sects. One of these was known as the 'Sweet Singers' although the name belies their beliefs. They were convinced that Edinburgh was destined to explode in a firestorm sent down from heaven and be consumed in the same way as Sodom and Gomorrah. Even odder is the fact that this was an all-female group who abandoned their children and husbands to their fate while they set out for a safe haven from which to watch the destruction of the city. The most interesting aspect, however, is that the place of sanctuary they chose was located on the Pentland Hills, although the exact site is unknown. It seems that the hills had a mystic significance for this group of believers and that they were convinced that staying on the Pentlands would save them from the fury that was about to engulf their fellow citizens. The disaster, of course, did not materialise and the women were eventually rounded up and returned home. But the fact that it was a female cult coupled with the strange form of the Pentland goddess suggests that they were either pulled unconsciously towards the Pentlands or had realised the significance of them for themselves. Is this further evidence that this area could have been, at one time, the site of the worship of a female goddess? The mystic *Cailleach*?

It's certainly strange that a Christian chapel like Rosslyn should lie almost in the shadow of a range of hills which may have been dedicated to a pagan goddess. But then Rosslyn is no ordinary place, as the many strange figures carved on its walls and ceilings testify. How is it that elaborate stone effigies of the Green Man, a pagan god of nature, are represented in this Christian sanctuary; one where it is said the Holy Grail, the ultimate Christian symbol, allegedly lies buried? In May 2006, yet another claim emerged about supposed secrets contained within the chapel. It was said that a scan of the crypt, carried out as far back as the 1980s, revealed eighteen graves. Sixteen of the bodies interred there had been buried in full armour which suggested they might be 'of royal blood'. It was also discovered that the area where the bodies had been buried had been covered with a layer of sand. It was argued that objects from King Solomon's temple had been hidden there and covered over to prevent anyone finding them. This followed the revelation that a metal detector had located an object, which some suggested had the appearance of a chalice, inside the famous 'apprentice pillar', the elaborately decorated buttress which dominates the interior of the chapel so spectacularly.

Rosslyn has become a sacred icon of such standing that even the head of Christ is alleged to have been buried there. But a UFO? Some have suggested that this is, in fact, the real secret of Rosslyn. That either an alien craft or information from alien visitors was hidden aeons ago beneath the ground on which the chapel now stands. This bold assertion could, of course, only be proved if, or when, the whole area is excavated. As this is unlikely to happen it has to be agreed that this can only rank as wide speculation, but may have its origins in what is undeniably true — that the balls of light, which are often seen in the area, have frequently been observed disappearing into the earth itself.

However, this is unlikely to have any connection to the strange underground tunnels that stretch from Rosslyn across the Esk Valley. There appears to be a sophisticated tunnel complex here, but no clear explanation as to what its purpose might have been. Some have linked the tunnels to claims that many sacred artefacts lie hidden in the area. But, whether or not these have any substance, it's clear that as far as these objects are concerned they are supposed to lie beneath the chapel itself. These strange tunnels appear to have a quite separate function and, I would suggest, may pre-date the construction of the chapel. It is possible that they were made for, and were used in, some type of mystic ceremonies. There's little doubt that in the early years of its development Christianity was very much mixed up with pagan beliefs. One key aspect of Druidism, for example, was the belief that the mystic and sacred realms existed below ground and could be visited through tunnels. Perhaps this offers an explanation for the existence of this mysterious cave system.

However, strange tunnels are not only, or even mainly, located round Rosslyn Chapel. There are several sites, even within the heart of the city, where tunnels exist and for which there is no obvious explanation. 'Gilmerton Cove' is one such place. As far back as 1845, as detailed in *The Third Statistical Account,* a national survey compiled by the Church of Scotland, there were doubts over the cave's history. At that time the authors wrote:

> There is at Gilmerton a singular cave, dug out of solid rocks.
> It contains several apartments and was finished in 1724 by an
> eccentric inhabitant of that place after five years hard labour.
> [He] lived with his family and carried on his occupation as a
> smith in the place till 1753.

The smith in question was George Paterson. As the world grew increasing rational and rejected mysticism, Gilmerton Cove was seen as nothing more than the creation of a local eccentric. However, it is worth noting that the lands on which the cave lay were at one time owned by the St Clairs; the family that built the mystical temple now famous as Rosslyn Chapel.

It may be true that the cave was used and extended by Paterson, but other evidence suggests that it dates from a much earlier period. It would seem unlikely that Paterson would have made use of anything other than an existing structure, though he may well have adapted it for his own purposes. Rumours and myths have attached themselves to the site. One is that it was used by the Knights Templar. Unless evidence emerges from somewhere then this can only remain as speculation, though it is true that the Templars did make use of this type of place to carry out secret rituals. The Templars have well-documented links to Rosslyn Chapel and it's possible that the cave system might have been used for initiation ceremonies of some kind. Freemasons may also have met there and, as the St Clairs at one time owned the land and have been linked to both organisations, it is possible that Gilmerton Cove did serve as a secret gathering place.

It has also been claimed that a tunnel system linked Gilmerton

Cove to Craigmillar Castle. There may be some truth in this though there has been no attempt to locate this underground complex and, therefore, at the moment it can be no more than an unproven legend. However, it is certainly true that this area did have mystical links. St Catherine's Well close by, was famous for its power to heal. It was claimed that many miraculous cures occurred there, and the waters were believed to be especially effective in dealing with skin diseases. An annual procession was made to the well in honour of St Catherine and it was so highly prized that even as protestant a monarch as James VI visited it in 1617, and ordered the well to be enclosed properly and protected.

The fascination with constructing caves and tunnels in order to engage in bizarre secret rituals continued well into the eighteenth century. Sir John Clerk of Penicuik, who had an obsession with the beliefs of the ancient world, had a shaft dug into the side of a hill on his estate. Half way down the tunnel he constructed a small room carved out of solid rock. Here, with the walls decorated with strange designs, Clerk and a group of initiates took part in rituals of some kind. Intriguingly, Clerk was a close friend of James St Clair and, in 1736, encouraged him to carry out repairs to Rosslyn Chapel after it had been damaged by mob violence some fifty years before. Clerk was a prominent freemason and 1736 was also the year that the Freemasons' Grand Lodge of Scotland was founded.

Strange unexplained tunnels continue to be discovered. In March 2009, tramworkers revealed three mysterious underground chambers on Princes Street, thought to date from the eighteenth century, although their use is still unknown. It's said that more vaults have been discovered beneath the North and South Bridge, and I have been assured on several occasions that a tunnel exists linking Calton Hill to Arthur's Seat; one that runs beneath the site of the present Scottish parliament.

Like Rome, Edinburgh is said to have been built on seven hills and each site can claim to be linked to paranormal events. Arthur's Seat has certainly been a focus for many bizarre incidents stretching from distant centuries down to the present day. But was 'Arthur's Seat' so named because of a link to the legendary king? Certainly Edinburgh and the surrounding area can boast several sites with a historical connection, whether real or mythical, to Arthur. The name 'Arthur's Seat' need not be taken to imply that Arthur lived in the area, although one legend holds that Arthur was buried here and will one day return. Similar legends connect Arthur to areas not too far away. The Eildon Hills also boasts a tradition that King Arthur lies in a grave surrounded by his knights. It may be that what we are talking about is an idea, a religious symbolism that focused on particular hill sites because of ceremonies or long-standing myths associated with them. One key fact that has become clear in recent years is that Arthur was linked to the Scottish lowlands as strongly as with the south of England or Wales. And his key advisor, the man possessed of supernatural powers, Merlin, is more strongly associated with the Scottish lowlands than elsewhere in Britain.

Other evidence has suggested that Arthur was active in the area. There's the well-known 'Arthur's o'en' in nearby Stenhousemuir; an oval, stone-built building, now demolished, said to have been built in this shape to house King Arthur's famous round table. And to add to that, Camelon in Falkirk is one of the sites suggested for the great battle of the same name, one of the six battles fought by Arthur against the invading Angles and Saxons. As has been pointed out by writer Alistair Moffat, several sites in the Borders have an Arthurian association and Merlin is also said to have died and been buried at Drumelzier. Put together with the Edinburgh links it does suggest that Arthur was strongly associated with an area extending down from the Firth of Forth which had Edinburgh as its focus.

It has even been suggested that the final resting place of King Arthur, the Avalon of legend, was located in the Firth of Forth on the Isle of May. Whether or not King Arthur really existed may be irrelevant in this respect. It is certainly possible that these legends arose around Edinburgh because the area had such a strong mystical aura. It was a place which seemed to act as a bridge between this world and other worlds.

Although the legends surrounding King Arthur exercised a powerful influence on the minds of our ancestors it is unlikely to have been a factor leading the Knights Templar to set up a base in Edinburgh, following their expulsion from France in 1307. It's more likely to have been a recognition that the area possessed a mystical atmosphere, a place where their secret rituals, damned as blasphemy in the rest of Europe, would blend into the aura and they could practise their beliefs without disturbance. It was maybe at this time that the close links between the St Clair family and the Knights Templar began to develop. Certainly, they have become entwined in tradition and both are linked to mystical sites across the city.

In December 1998, Edinburgh was hit by a severe storm and one casualty was an ancient sycamore tree which stood in Corstorphine. There were several strange legends linked to the tree. It was said to have been planted at the same time as building began on Rosslyn Chapel. This would have made it some five hundred years old which, on the face of it, appears unlikely. The normal life span for a sycamore tree is far less. However, there is at least a symbolic link between the two sites, as the St Clair family who built Rosslyn and the Forrester clan who owned areas of Corstorphine were, it is said, closely associated. This might explain one of the legends linked to the ancient sycamore. It is said that a hoard owned by the Knights Templar is buried beneath it, which is reminiscent of the claim that Templar treasure is buried beneath Rosslyn Chapel. It's not quite clear why these two sites should be connected in this way. It is possible that the sycamore stands at a spot that was once regarded as sacred, though it's a mystery why this should be the case.

However, the legend that a 'white lady' guards the spot and has appeared holding a sword dripping with blood indicates that there is a long tradition associated with the area, which pre-dates the growth of the sycamore. This materialisation of a white lady apparently defending the site, however, contrasts with a legend linked to Rosslyn that a 'green lady' will one day appear and reveal where Templar treasure is buried. White ladies are often linked to ancient wells, usually regarded as the haunt of spirits in ancient myth, and it is possible that, in the past a well once existed here or close by. In connection with this, it is interesting to note that, in folklore, a sycamore radiated energy of some kind that kept fairies at bay. There was also a tragic story linked to the Corstorphine sycamore. It's said that a daughter of one of the Forrester lairds fell in love with a man her father regarded as unsuitable. She met her boyfriend beneath the sycamore and it was here that her father found them together and killed him. She died of a broken heart and her phantom now haunts the site. However, this may have been an explanation given by later generations to account for the appearance of unearthly spirits.

There are other links connecting the St Clairs of Rosslyn to the Knights Templars. South of the Meadows where the area now known as Sciennes developed, there once stood a monastery, that of St Catherine of Scienna, which was run by Dominican nuns and founded by Lady St Clair of Rosslyn. Opposite this site, across the Meadows, a chapel of the Knights Templar was set on a slight rise. It was known as 'Mount Hooly', which has been interpreted as a later corruption of 'Holy Mount'. As far back as 1799, historian Hugo Arnot commented:

> As the Knights professed to defend the holy mount and sepulchre, and to protect pilgrims resorting to it, this branch of them, in commemoration of the grand object of their order had bestowed on the site of the chapel the name of the 'Holy Mount'. In digging the ground some time ago, several bodies were found there, buried cross-legged and having swords by their sides.

This raises a number of questions. Why was this site viewed as so sacred? Did it house some relic that was regarded as of such importance that it deserved the designation 'Holy Mount?' It may also be the case that there was a 'holy way' which stretched from the site of Rosslyn Chapel into the centre of the city, by way of the 'Holy Mount', and ended at the foot of the Royal Mile. It was here, with Arthur's Seat as a backdrop, that a mystical incident took place which impacted on the history of a city and, indeed, on Scotland.

On 14 September 1128, King David I was holding his court in the Castle of Edinburgh. It was the day of the Feast of the Elevation of the Cross, but instead of passing the day in solemn observance David decided that he would rather go hunting. The area lying around the castle and towards Arthur's Seat was heavily forested at this time and a favourite hunting ground for the king as it was full of game, including deer. The hunting party passed from the Castle down to the East , but when the hunters came below Salisbury Crags the king found himself separated from his courtiers. It is possible that at this point the king entered some mystical realm as he found himself confronted by an enormous white stag.

The king's horse, startled, tried to gallop away, but the hart

*The stags head emblem of the Canongate burgh. It commemorates
a mystic encounter experienced by King David I in 1128.*

charged and threw the horse and rider to the ground wounding David in the thigh. The king, half-stunned, raised his arm to shield himself from a further thrust of the stag's horns, but found that his hand clutched not antlers but a crucifix made from part of the very cross to which Jesus had been nailed. David kept a tight hold on the cross and the white stag gradually vanished before his eyes. Overwhelmed by this experience, the king returned to the castle and, to commemorate this strange event, decreed that Holyrood Abbey would be built on the spot where the pieces of the true cross had been placed in his hand. The Canongate coat of arms still shows the stag's head with a cross between the horns, in remembrance of this event. There is certainly at least one odd aspect to this tale. The stag is an ancient pagan symbol as it bears horns which represent the gods of nature. So it's puzzling why a portion of the Christian cross should emerge from the antlers of such as animal. However, whatever the reality, the upshot was that the site where Holyrood Abbey was created was, from then on, viewed as one of the city's most sacred sites.

So does that explain why a new building for the first Scottish parliament in nearly three hundred years was erected close to King David's mystical encounter? It seems an odd coincidence. And what makes its selection all the more odd was that it was by no means the front runner as the location. Other sites appeared more practical and it was a shock when, out of nowhere, the Holyrood spot was chosen. What was equally strange was that the person who was determined that this would be the place where it should be built was the Glaswegian MP Donald Dewar, the first-ever 'First Minister' in Scotland's new parliament. Donald Dewar was seen as a man with a real down-to-earth and practical approach to life; not the kind of person to have an interest in the mystical side. An interpretation that proved mistaken. After his death it emerged that Dewar had not only amassed a two-million-pound fortune, but that he had gathered a collection of Scottish colourist paintings worth over £400,000. More significant than the value, however, was the fact that the painters attached to this style were linked to the Celtic Revival in Scottish art, which took place in the early years of the last century. They were interested in mystical themes and frequently visited Iona, viewed as an enchanted isle where supernatural entities were reportedly seen, encounters experienced by the artists themselves. Dewar was undoubtedly aware of the historical importance of the location he chose describing it as a, 'site at the heart of so much Scottish History.' It was certainly not for practical reasons that Donald Dewar set his own heart on Holyrood. As Scottish National Party leader, Alex Salmond, put it: 'Donald Dewar seems to have an enormous attachment to personally creating a new piece of architecture for future generations.'

To add to the mystery, the architect, Enrico Miralles, put together a design so strange that it baffled, and continues to baffle, all alike. Some compared it to an upturned boat. On the other hand, when viewed from above, some claimed it had the appearance of a pyramid. To others it resembled the 'all seeing eye' of the god Horus, a motif strongly linked to ancient Egypt, but which also appears in various modern guises including, as is well known, the US one-dollar bill. It would be curious if Scotland's alleged connection with the land of the Pharaohs had resurfaced in the technology obsessed era of the twenty-first century.

Apart from having a strange appearance, the parliament building also cost ten times its original budget to build and is, as experience has shown, expensive to maintain. So why wasn't a building more straightforward in design, cheaper to build and a more suitable location chosen? Dewar may have been obsessed with the area, but were there other forces at work? Unseen, mystical currents?

Does the answer lie in the power of ley lines? Leys are invisible streams of energy which run in straight lines across the country. Their existence and purpose remains controversial. However, whatever they may be, they definitely appear to exist and can be detected using dowsing rods. Dowsing, using metal or wooden rods to detect objects, is also controversial even though it is regularly employed to find water, oil and minerals, and is used by individuals from archaeologists to electricians to pipe layers. As it is regarded as 'unscientific' no one likes to admit to making use of it, but our ancestors were certainly aware of it as every ancient standing-stone circle has, as dowsers have shown, several ley lines running through it. It seems that thousands of years ago people recognised instinctively where this underground energy flowed and built their monuments to connect with them.

This might explain why Arthur's Seat has a long history as a site with mystical significance. Prehistoric man established many settlements here and began a long tradition of spiritual association with it that continues to the present. In ancient times it was a centre for the worship of the god Lug. It was also the site of later Beltane fire festivals, a tradition which can still be seen in the May Day ritual of climbing the hill. It has a reputation as a place where it is possible to cross from this world to the next, and is peppered with mystic sites, from 'fairy knowes' to the medieval St Anthony's Chapel built by the Knights Templar. In modern times, it became a focus for UFO sightings.

Arthur's Seat, my investigation has revealed, is the focus for ley lines spreading out across the capital. Several pass through the area where the Scottish parliament now stands. When the site of the parliament was under discussion I, following a request from a newspaper and for a BBC programme, dowsed the Holyrood Site, Calton Hill and an area in Leith, all of which were being proposed as potential locations. I found that Holyrood was by far the most active in terms of leys as it was located so close to Arthur's Seat. I suggested that because of this it might be better to place it elsewhere as the effect of streams of ley energy is unpredictable. Some have argued that they are beneficial others suggest that they can be harmful. All those involved in the investigation of these issues agree, however, that they have an effect on the individual.

Officials in the UK might be sceptical about the impact of ley lines and 'earth energy', but the same isn't true in other countries. Chinese interest in feng shui is well known, but countries nearer home have also displayed a more open attitude to the influence of these invisible energy streams. You could hardly view Austria and Germany as countries with their heads in the clouds. Indeed, they are generally viewed as extraordinarily level-headed and practical. So if the citizens here take these aspects seriously should we be so determined to scoff at them? The city of Innsbruck, in the heart of Austria, has revealed a willingness to accept that invisible streams of energy — ley lines — run across the city and can influence their lives. In a town park located in the heart of the medieval quarter stands a well-maintained monument. It was a present to the citizens of Innsbruck following a feng shui conference held in the city in 2000. The inscription on the monument reads: 'The energy stone marks the lung point of the city of Innsbruck. An important energy point, it improves the energy flow and enhances energy potential in the city of Innsbruck.' The inscription appears in Italian and German too.

But controlling this energy flow is also seen as a potential benefit. In 2003, Druids were recruited in an effort to reduce accidents on Austria's roads. A three-hundred-metre stretch on the A9 route through Styria was a particular accident black spot. Leading Druid, Gerald Knobloch, claimed that he had 'located dangerous elements that had disrupted the energy flow.' The solution was to restore the energy balance in the area by erecting two quartz stones, each weighing a ton, at the side of the road. There was a fall in the number of accidents. This will come as no surprise to those who dowse earth energies. It seems that they can have an impact on mental perception. As far back as the 1920s, Germans were conducting official investigations into the impact of underground energy flow on people in homes and offices. Buildings were sited to take account of the pathway of leys, especially where they intersected.

Could the architects and movers and shakers of Edinburgh

have been influenced in the same way, without being consciously aware of it? Are there strange forces in the aura that surrounds us, or beneath the earth, that lead human minds to create patterns in the landscape? How else can we explain the bizarre findings of David Ovason, discoveries which I can confirm are echoed in the layout of Edinburgh itself.

In 2000, David Ovason published a ground breaking book called *The Secret Zodiacs of Washington DC*, subtitled *Was the City of Stars planned by Masons?* It detailed an intensive investigation of the layout of the US capital and has been the subject of widespread comment and several television documentaries. Following years of researching the streets and building of Washington, a project which covered the two hundred years since its foundation, David Ovason came to a startling conclusion. Its architects and planners had built into the city's layout, either deliberately or unconsciously, a range of figures representing the zodiacal constellation of Virgo. These had been incorporated in buildings, ceiling decorations, fountains and statues, among others. Most puzzling of all, however, Ovason demonstrated convincingly that the layout of streets in the heart of the city also form a diagrammatical representation of Virgo. How could this have come about?

Such figures are not unknown in the UK. As far back as the 1930s, it was claimed that in the area surrounding Glastonbury Tor in Somerset the full range of zodiac figures, including Leo, Aries and Gemini, were outlined in the landscape by hills, streams, woods and lanes. When viewed together from above these features are seen to make out an individual diagrammatic zodiac, just as Davd Ovason later discovered can be found in Washington DC.

I was fascinated by the idea of the Glastonbury Earth Zodiac, and, unaware of David Ovason's project, wondered if such configurations might exist at 'sacred spots' elsewhere. Edinburgh, of course, sprang to mind. During the 1980s, I spent many hours walking the streets of the capital and the surrounding countryside, examining street layouts and looking at the formation of hills and watercourses. I scrutinised photographs taken from above the city and looked at city maps going back centuries. Eventually, I identified several zodiac shapes, which we normally associate with the sky, could be found formed on the ground in and around Edinburgh.

The most prominent is the figure of Aquarius as he dominates the central area of the city. The figure is formed by the outline of roads and other features which give us the shape of a man holding, as befits the 'water carrier', a large container. Examining a modern map of the city it can be seen that the brow of Aquarius's head is formed by the line of Princes Street. One side of the face is outlined by Lothian Road and the North Bridge on the other. The line of the jaw is formed by the Meadows with, incidentally, its well-known 'Jaw Bone Walk'. To the west, the neck and body can be followed down the A702 to Fairmilehead, and on the east down the A701 to Liberton. An outstretched arm reaches to the town of Dalkeith, formed on the outer side by the A68 to Sheriffhall, and the inner side by the A7, from Nether Liberton to Edinburgh. The hand is formed by the continuation of these two roads to Eskbank. The North Esk River runs through the water carrier's outstretched hand.

The existence of such a figure seems to defy common sense and I admit that I have to examine it each time afresh to convince myself that it is really there. How could such a figure be formed, which in any case is only visible when looked at from a considerable height or on a map? Has it something to do with the resurgence of Scotland? Is it a coincidence that we have recently moved from the zodiacal Age of Pisces and entered the Age of Aquarius; the very period which has seen the emergence of a more nationally aware Scotland and the setting up of the country's own parliament? Can there be any connection? Perhaps the appearance of Aquarius in the heart of the city somehow reflects what is taking place in the minds and souls of the citizens of Edinburgh. Whatever the answer, the mystery of the city's landscape and how it came to be formed, and is still forming, will be, no doubt, an endless topic for debate.

But Edinburgh's mystic aura can produce rather more direct and disturbing effects. Effects that impact on the individual in a variety of bizarre ways. The capital, at times, appears to be awash with reports of poltergeists, ghosts, aliens beings and vampires. A range of the entities that, among others, appear to haunt the streets and buildings of the city. Unfortunately for the inhabitants these spectres from the 'other world' seem to find the 'Athens of the North' a very attractive place indeed. There are those who will remain sceptical. But as the following chapters will reveal the sheer number of weird incidents recorded, and the first hand witness accounts, is surely proof enough that Edinburgh can justly lay claim to the title of the world's strangest capital. It's hard to think of another city that can even remotely compete.

2

Poltergeists

Is there any difference between a ghost and a poltergeist? A ghost can appear in many forms and seeing one can undoubtedly prove a disturbing experience, particularly if, as psychics claim, he or she is the spirit of a deceased person. We don't expect to encounter the dead and it can come as a shock to confront the phantom of someone who may be long-buried. Ghosts, however, normally show little interest in their surroundings and may appear quite unaware of them, but it is an entirely different matter with the poltergeist. Here we have an entity which appears to interact with the environment, who seems to demand attention and may quite deliberately set out to frighten and disturb us.

Even so a poltergeist's activities vary and often start with incidents which appear, on the face of it, trivial. In February 1989, I was called in to investigate events at Coasters Disco, situated in Tollcross. Staff had been disturbed by a series of strange incidents and were looking for an explanation for what was taking place. The dance club occupied three floors of an old building. On the ground floor was the 'Outer Limits' disco. The floor above was occupied by the 'Bermuda Triangle' and the one above that was known as the 'Barbados Suite'. They were connected by a main staircase, which was used by customers to move from one hall to another. A second narrower stairway, used only by staff, ran from the bar located in the Barbados Suite all the way down to the ground floor. These were the only two ways by which it was possible to get from one part of the building to another, so neither staff nor anyone else could move about the premises without being noticed. As everyone was on the alert, and someone playing tricks would have been easily spotted, it seemed to rule out human agency as the cause. But what was going on?

Management of the club first became aware that a poltergeist had been activated in the building when the cleaners refused to work alone on the premises, following a succession of odd events. One morning, as staff prepared to clean the floor of the Barbados Suite, a vacuum cleaner of a heavy industrial kind that was used every day, and always functioned normally, suddenly started moving around the room all by itself. What really jangled the cleaners' nerves was that the machine hadn't even been plugged in, let alone switched on. As the vacuum cleaner carried out a bizarre 'dance' around the room coloured lights suspended from the ceiling started flashing on and off, as if an invisible spirit was playing some kind of strange game.

But this was only the most bizarre of a succession of inexplicable incidents which had stretched over several weeks. At the end of each night glasses were washed then stacked on the shelves behind the bar. In the morning several would be found in pieces, lying on the ground as if they had been deliberately knocked to the floor. There appeared no way that this could happen in any normal manner and it seemed especially odd as, over previous months, they had all remained safely in place. The glass-breaking incidents had started literally overnight as if some malevolent switch had been thrown. Other incidents were as unsettling as they were trivial. Bottles of whisky were moved around the bar overnight and even items like cleaning cloths and liquids would be found in a different spot from where they'd been left when staff had gone home.

It was hard to put these events down simply to chance as they formed a pattern, and the overall picture suggested that a weird force of some kind had been activated, though why this should suddenly come about was hard to explain. Doors were heard opening and closing as if an invisible force was moving through the building. Pools of water formed on the floor of the Barbados Suite out of nowhere; a well-known mark of poltergeist activity and seen frequently as an indication of the presence of a force from another dimension.

Typical of the poltergeist phenomenon were scratching noises heard by cleaning staff. It's not known why these sounds should be caused by this spirit, but they nearly always seem to occur. The disturbances, however, went beyond these strange incidents and the poltergeist made its presence felt in even more unsettling ways. Female screams echoed through the building when it was known to be empty. However, the phantom that manifested itself, seen by several cleaners early one morning, appeared to be definitely that of a man. It materialised while staff were enjoying a smoke break in the Bermuda Triangle hall. The door connecting the room to the bar above slowly opened and a dark figure appeared then vanished. It was seen quite clearly in the mirrors that ran all the way round the room. Frightening, certainly, but puzzling too. Was this phantom really the cause of so many odd events? And if so why?

A psychic medium, Joan Davidson, after contacting the 'other side' suggested that the spirit of a twenty-year-old man was at the root of the problem. He claimed that he had died in a fire where the disco building now stood. On the other hand, a member of staff, Margaret, using her psychic abilities was convinced that the spirit was that of a young woman who was killed on the site. I have been unable to confirm that either event took place, but that is not to say that they didn't have a basis in fact. However, my investigation of the poltergeist phenomenon over the last twenty years has convinced me that any message received where this phenomenon occurs has, by its very nature, to be doubted. 'Poltergeist' means a noisy and mischievous spirit and there can be no doubt that wherever it comes from, and whatever it may be, it sets out deliberately to confuse, annoy and frighten.

A poltergeist invading a house or active in a cemetery might be understandable, but would such a spirit take over a lump of metal? Or a vehicle? In November 2002, railway crew working on a track near the Craigentinny depot were startled to receive an emergency phone call. Officials at Waverley station warned them that a driverless train was heading straight for them. With only seconds to spare the thirty-man team jumped clear of the lines as the engine, weighing a bone-crushing 103 tons, hurtled past them. At 3.30 a.m. on a pitch-dark morning they would never have seen it coming and there's little doubt that without that phone call several men might have been badly injured. So what had happened? The train with no one in the cab had pulled out of its siding and moved slowly, some might say, almost stealthily, along the track, gradually building up speed. It's estimated that by the time it had travelled the three miles to Craigentinny it had reached twenty miles an hour, fast enough to cause a disaster which was only averted after the train, a class 80 electric locomotive hired to pull the Highlander Sleeper service, was turned on to a siding, still driverless. Railway experts have had a century and a half of building safety into train engines and each locomotive is packed full of failsafe devices, so how could a modern train move off all on its own? Naturally, 'mechanical failure' was the explanation favoured by officials, but how many trains do you read of starting up without a driver present? None, thankfully, apart from this one. So could some poltergeist, intent on causing havoc, have interfered with the controls? Or did some entity invade the very engine itself and furnish it with a malevolent will of its own?

Individuals may experience an event suggestive of poltergeist activity, but which goes no further than a one-off incident. In the 1980s, Lynn was sitting in her flat in Dundas Street drinking a cup of coffee. She was holding the mug tightly in her hand when, suddenly, it shot from her grasp in a straight line, feet above the floor, to hit the opposite wall, where it broke into pieces. Lynn was shocked and could think of no reason to explain what had happened. It never occurred again. In 2006, Euan, a student, was living in a flat in Arden Street where, from time to time, he would hear the sounds of a woman singing operatic songs. The voice, which had an unearthly quality, seemed to come from the flat below and the singing, which would last only a few minutes at a time, broke out with no obvious pattern. The incidents struck him as strange and out of place in a building which was occupied mainly by students at this time. In 1988, Caitlin, then a teenager, was alone in the cottage where she was staying on an estate near South Queensferry. She was off school on this particular day because she had not been feeling well and was lying in bed with the covers pulled up. Suddenly, she felt a weight across her legs as if someone had crept up silently and lain across them. Petrified, she was too scared to move, but as nothing more happened she looked up gingerly over the covers only to discover that there was no one there. As in Lynn's experience, nothing odd happened after this. But what these incidents, among many others, do suggest is that poltergeist phenomena are more frequent than is imagined or reported. They are overlooked simply because they do not develop into a full-blown poltergeist infestation. If we knew the reason why we might be nearer to explaining what type of spirit we are dealing with.

So how seriously should we take the poltergeist phenomenon? Those with an interest in the 'world beyond' have found themselves unable to ignore it. In May 1974, the General Assembly of the Church of Scotland set up a working party with the aim of examining, 'the results of the recent experiments in the field of Parapsychology, paying particular attention to those which might have some bearing on the present day understanding and good expression of the Christian faith.' Over the next two years, the committee examined 'card-guessing experiments, emotions in plants [anticipating Prince Charles], Uri Geller,' among others, and exorcism. It issued its report in May 1976. The committee didn't come to any definite conclusion with regard to parapsychology, but on exorcism its advice was quite specific. It recommended that:

> Ministers of the Church of Scotland should be enjoined from conducting a special ceremony of Exorcism. We recommend that any person encountering a case of alleged 'possession' should refer it to a physician and should remain in consultation with him as to treatment thereafter.

On the face of it this seemed to suggest that, though poltergeist and possession may not be identical phenomena, they are closely linked and that, therefore, the Working Party did not accept that poltergeist manifestations had any basis in fact.

This, however, had not always been the church's attitude and, even in 1974, this may not have been the unanimous view of the clergy. In the winter of 1959, a house was so badly affected by poltergeist activity that a Church of Scotland minister was called in to cleanse the house of the infestation. The building was situated in Winton Terrace, Fairmilehead, and was occupied by Baroness Kilbride. The minister who carried out the exorcism was the Reverend J.W. Stevenson who was at the time well known as the editor of the Church of Scotland's official magazine *Life and Work*.

The kind of phenomenon that was experienced was typical of the effects linked to the poltergeist. The sounds of heavy objects crashing to the floor echoed through the rooms, but when the noises were investigated there was nothing obvious to explain the disturbance. Doors opened and closed by themselves when there was no one present. Articles were moved from one room to another including a pair of binoculars which, having been placed in an upstairs room, was somehow transported to a table on the ground floor while all five occupants of the house were huddled together on the stairs.

It appears that the Reverend Stevenson recognised that, 'there was . . . some kind of spirit presence,' but that 'it was a very obscure phenomenon.' A view which anyone who has dealt with poltergeist activity would wholeheartedly endorse. He denied that his attempt to end the phenomenon was an exorcism. However, it appears to have been that in all but name as he said a prayer 'for the deliverance of any spirit chained and held to this life.' Remarkably, the prayer appeared to work and the strange incidents which had gone on for some time stopped. This may have been coincidence, but, psychics say that if an effort is made to communicate with the poltergeist who, it has been suggested, may be a spirit which refuses to move on, then making contact can persuade the entity to leave the place to which it is attached.

Of course, others take a less sanguine view of the poltergeist phenomenon and doubt that appeals to the entity's good nature can have any effect. Poltergeists, in my experience, reveal a degree of cunning and devious behaviour that can certainly challenge the view that we are dealing simply with a 'lost' or 'playful' spirit. Events in Greyfriars Kirkyard could be evidence for that.

On 28 October 2009, I visited Greyfriars Kirkyard in the company of well-known Scottish medium Gary Gray. Gary has earned a reputation as a psychic who can furnish detailed information provided by the spirits of the dead. Given that much has been written regarding poltergeist activity in the graveyard, I wanted to see what he would make of it all. I should say that though I had visited Greyfriars Kirk in the past, and even attended a wedding there in the 1970s, I had not personally been aware of any paranormal activity and had seen it purely as a site of historic interest. In the 1980s, however, when I was conducting various psychic investigations across the city I was told of an incident at Greyfrairs that had taken place as far back as the 1960s.

Louise Ross had been visiting Greyfriars Kirk in the company of her then boyfriend David. He was not from Edinburgh and so Louise was taking him round various places of interest and, having visited the Chambers Street Museum, walked him up to see the grave of Greyfriars Bobby. From there they wandered further into the cemetery. David found it quite interesting and went from grave to grave searching for the names of well-known figures. Louise, less interested, lagged behind and at one point David disappeared out of sight having headed towards the Flodden Wall. As Louise stood waiting for him to return she spotted a figure in the distance. He seemed to be staring at her. It made Louise feel a bit uncomfortable and she looked around hoping that David was coming back towards her, but he was still out of sight. She was trying to ignore the figure standing at the graveside, happy at least that there was a good gap between them, but somehow she could not help glancing at it. As she did so she noticed that it was moving towards her and, what was more disturbing, not only appeared to be glowing which she hadn't noticed before, but floating slightly above the ground. Louise admits that as this was in November the light was fading, not because it was late in the afternoon, but because the sky was becoming heavily overcast with dark cloud, so the figure was not as clear as it might have been. She is adamant though that this is what she saw. Louise explained, 'I was transfixed to the spot. I couldn't believe what I was seeing. I wanted to run and shout for David, but I seemed just frozen.' The figure kept moving towards her and just when she thought it was going to come right up to her it simply vanished in an instant.

But Louise's relief was short-lived for a moment later she felt a sharp tug on the back of her hair as if someone was trying to pull her round. Immediately she thought of David, but when she turned about there was no one there. This was too much for Louise who found her voice and 'screamed for David to come' as she put it. David ran over and found Louise white and shaking. She said:

> I tried to explain what had happened, but I was just jabbering. But I think he guessed that something odd had occurred and we got out of there double fast. When I had calmed down I told him about it. I don't know if he believed me though.

Louise added that she had never had any supernatural experiences previously and hadn't had one since. The incident at Greyfriars Kirk had been a one-off.

I'm not sure why, at the time this was related to me in the 1980s, I did not take it more seriously. Louise was not sure exactly where the event had occurred though she thought it was at the lower slope of the graveyard, which would have taken it away from the site of George Mackenzie's mausoleum and the Covenanters' Prison where many strange incidents have recently been reported. I did go as far as visiting the cemetery

The Covenanter's prison at Greyfriar's Kirk. Scene of terrifying poltergeist activity.

accompanied by a friend who was a psychic some months after first hearing Louise's story, but nothing of real significance was picked up. I was surprised, therefore, when Greyfrairs hit the headlines as a spot where poltergeist manifestations seemed to have exploded into a 'hot spot' of activity. On reflection, however, it can be seen that this fits the pattern of such events. There seems to be a burst of such incidents which may last for a few days, months or, in some cases, years, but then things quieten down. It may be that the graveyard will fit this model, though given the interest in the events there, it is possible that the entities involved will feed off this and somehow sustain their presence for some considerable time.

This time, with Gary Gray present, I was determined to carry out a more thorough investigation and while Gary was in contact with the spirits I dowsed using my diving rods. I have found through several years' experience that the rods can be used for many different purposes and react in those areas where spirits have been active. As we walked together through the graveyard it was astonishing how both Gary and I, using different abilities, got very similar results. The rods went haywire at the sloping, south side of the kirkyard, and Gary confirmed that there was intense spirit activity in this area. On the other side, on the slope overlooking the church, it was very quiet. I have to say that I have never experienced such a different result in a single enclosed space like this. The church itself was the dividing line which appeared to mark the boundary between one very active spirit area and one very quiet one. But here is the most bizarre aspect of it all. The 'quiet area' was where the mausoleum of George Mackenzie is located; one area where it has been reported people have experienced intense poltergeist activity. So why did Gary not pick up 'signals' at such a spot? Gary told me, 'If there were spirits here they would contact me.' I have to agree as Gary undoubtedly possesses a very high degree of psychic ability.

Personally, I found this unnerving. It suggested to me that either the area had somehow been swept clean of spirit activity. Or that some powerful force was deliberately blocking spirit communication and simply did not want anyone to make contact with Gary. But how and why could that happen? Was it afraid of what might be revealed to such a powerful medium?

Gary, who lives in Glasgow, had not previously visited Greyfriars Kirk. What made this an even more interesting visit for him was that his mother had been born in Candlemaker Row, which runs down the side of the graveyard, so it was a

*George Mackenzie's mausoleum at Greyfriar's Kirk. Does
Mackenzie's spirit still prowl the graveyard and cause
the strange phenomena experienced here, as has been claimed?*

rather poignant moment for Gary as it was the first time that
he had seen that as well. As soon as Gary walked past the
entrance gate into the cemetery the spirits seemed to come

rushing to him. 'I'm getting the name "John Gray,"' he told me after only a few steps inside. 'I'm being pulled in this direction.' I followed Gary down a side path looking at the names on the gravestone as we walked. He pulled up suddenly. 'I'm getting the name very strongly here.' I stopped too and looked around. Then almost fell backwards in astonishment. There on the marker directly behind Gary was the name 'John Gray'. I know for a fact Gary was completely unaware, as was I, that this was the name of the owner of the legendary Skye terrier 'Greyfriars Bobby'. It was amazing confirmation of Gary's psychic skills.

We continued in a similar way for the next few hours with Gary repeatedly mentioning names which we discovered on tombstones with the details Gary had indicated. One was a lady called 'Jessica' who appeared to Gary in an old-fashioned dress which he thought might have been of an eighteenth-century design. Gary explained that she kept coming to the cemetery because her husband was buried here and she still could not get over his death. He also saw two young children, a brother and sister, who used to play near the bottom entrance to the kirkyard.

During the time that we were there Gary was unaware of any feelings of evil, of the kind that produced the assaults on individuals that have been reported. I asked Gary that, if there was nothing evil present, who or what was the entity who was touching and frightening people who came there? He replied, 'there is the spirit of a man present who used to spend his time tending the graveyard. He resents people coming into the cemetery and is trying to get them to go away.' Could that explain the poltergeist? An entity which resents the presence of others? It certainly fits with the experience of some.

In the 1950s, events at Hazeldean Terace in Gilmerton attracted nationwide attention. Over a three-year period,

Hazeldean terrace. Peaceful today, but fifty years ago the street was the focus of a series of weird events.

starting in 1954, a couple, Mr and Mrs Currie, had experienced many instances of poltergeist activity in the house they then occupied. They were typical of the bizarre and often seemingly pointless activities of these 'noisy spirits'. Every Wednesday when the kitchen lay empty the wooden cover for their sink, which, as one observer noted, was ' tight and flush fitting and could not be moved without a strong pull', was lifted by an invisible hand out of its place and hurled with considerable force to the floor. The resulting crash would echo like the thunder of an express train through the building. In other incidents a watch-glass, tumbler and record player lying on the draining board were smashed to bits. 'I used to go upstairs to bed,' Mrs Currie explained, 'leaving these objects in the kitchen. When I came down in the morning they were broken. Oddly, the tumbler, a thick Jacobean type, had not disintegrated, even though it landed on the concrete of the kitchen floor. It was broken clean in half.'

In 1954, reporters from the *Evening Dispatch* newspaper conducted an experiment in the kitchen. It was an attempt to photograph the poltergeist in action and prove that this was no trick carried out by human agency. A string was attached from the board fitted over the sink to the trigger mechanism of the camera. If it moved the camera would be set off and whoever or whatever moved it would be caught on film. The door to the kitchen was then locked and the investigators who were alone in the house waited to see what happened next.

At three in the morning a loud bang, as if wood was being hit by a heavy object, echoed from the kitchen. As the reporters described it, 'We rushed into the room and found . . . nothing. The noise had stopped as suddenly as it had started.' However, the evidence that an inexplicable event had occurred was there for all to see. A tumbler which had split almost in two lay on the linoleum. A rug had been lifted up and lay in a heap beneath the bunker. It seemed as if the only reasonable explanation for the events lay in the realm of the paranormal. It appears, however, that nothing that could explain the incident was caught on film.

As is often the case, there seemed to be no obvious reason as to why the house at Hazeldean Terrace had been subjected to these mysterious series of events. According to Mrs Currie, 'When I first heard the strange noises I was frightened to tell my husband in case he laughed at me. But when he experienced them himself he was forced to take it seriously.' Mr Currie said:

> One day, when I was off ill and upstairs in bed, I heard banging
> in the kitchen. I rushed downstairs and everything was suddenly

quiet. The door to the hall and kitchen were both wide open and the rugs were thrown into a bundle. I shut the doors and tidied up the room and then went back to bed. No sooner was I beneath the covers when the noise started again.

When he investigated he found the doors again flung wide open and the rugs in a heap.

Again, as often happens, the activity fluctuated over time. By 1957, Mrs Currie could report that:

The noises and breaking of crockery are less frequent now. Maybe once a month, sometimes twice now. Apart from the continued breaking of my china it does us no harm. I prefer not to meddle with the spirits and things I do not understand. It's all better left alone.

She explained that the couple were not worried for themselves, but they didn't want their children to be upset by the events.

The events at Hazeldean Terrace eventually petered out. But had the poltergeist simply moved on to another location? In September 1958, the Van Horne family found themselves the target of unwanted and unexpected activity. According to one account, they had purchased some second-hand furniture, which they were told had belonged to a sailor who had died recently, and was being sold off at a bargain price. However, according to another account, the object which seemed to have caused so much trouble was acquired in a more puzzling way. It seems that a relative from the north of Scotland sent the family a piece of wood which had been rescued from a ruined cottage. They had, it seems, some kind of sentimental connection with the place though exactly what is unclear. Perhaps the purchase of furniture coincided with the arrival of the mysterious piece of wood and, in retrospect, the two events became linked in some way.

Whatever the truth, the various items of furniture, chairs and a sideboard, were taken back to the Van Horne residence at number 5, Rothesay Place. It wasn't long before the furniture began to take on a life of its own. Tapping noises could be heard. Ornaments placed on the furniture were found to have moved by themselves or were discovered lying on the floor. The family noticed a smell of tobacco smoke in the house which could not be accounted for. Neighbours complained of knocking through the kitchen wall when there was no one in the house. Family members watched on several occasions as the drawers on the dressing table opened and shut all by themselves. This was certainly evidence that a poltergeist had invaded the house, but what happened after was quite strange. The day following the dressing-table incident, Mrs Van Horne decided to burn the mysterious chunk of wood that had been sent from up north. Doing this certainly seemed to trigger something as the following morning the neighbours beneath her flat asked her what on earth she had been up to. They had been disturbed all night by a persistent knocking in the area of her fireplace.

There does seem evidence, however, that 'something' was present in the house. This entity, according to Mrs Van Horne, appeared as a shimmering circle of light which moved about the walls and responded when spoken to; the shimmering increased in intensity as if an effort was being made to communicate. A ball of light is believed by psychics to be a spirit or being from another world and so, though Mrs Van Horne labelled it 'Tinkerbell', it could have been anything but harmless. One thing is quite clear from the many reports of poltergeist activity, these entities pretend to be many things, from angels to demons, and manifest themselves in many forms, in fact, any shape they choose to.

Exactly what causes a poltergeist to become active is unclear. Would such an entity erupt because of an incident thousands of miles away? Would 'it', whatever 'it' is, be incensed because an object had been removed and taken to a new location? That objects appear somehow to attract entities from other worlds is confirmed in the notorious events surrounding Sir Alexander Seton. Seton no doubt thought that it was a bit of a coup to have been able to purchase and then bring home, in 1936, a piece of bone from a tomb of a pharaoh buried at Giza in Egypt. Within a matter of months he was to bitterly regret it. Over the following year, his wife, Lady Seton, suffered two serious illnesses and Alexander Seton was similarly brought down by ill health. It had all started innocently enough as Seton recalled:

> We were on holiday in Egypt and invited to accompany an official party at the opening of a new pharaoh's tomb from 3,000 BC. It had never been entered since that time. My wife thought it would be nice to have a memento and asked if she could have a piece of bone to take away. Removing objects is strictly forbidden and an official warned her not to in case anything untoward happened. She thought this a joke and was given a piece of bone.

The object was kept in a glass case in the dining room of their house at Learmonth Gardens. The bone was described as 'honeycombed with age and as light as a feather.' It certainly looked innocuous, but it had not been in its place for long when unexplained fires broke out in the building on two separate occasions. Phantoms started to appear and several witnesses described seeing a robed figure pacing the floors at night. A nine-year-old boy staying with the family woke them all one night shrieking with terror. When they went to investigate he was cowering under the bed clothes. He told them that he had gone to the bathroom and on the way had seen a figure clothed in 'a big dressing gown going into the living room.' When Sir Alexander went to investigate there was no one there.

However, Sir Alexander claimed that the incident could not be put down to the boy's imagination. He explained:

A woman friend of ours also saw this figure. She heard someone walking about during the night and thinking it was my wife came out of her room. She saw the figure disappearing into the drawing-room. She followed and saw it standing at the table on which the bone rests. When she switched on the light it disappeared.

The Setons decided to get rid of the bone and gave it to a surgeon friend believing that he would be too clear-headed to be unnerved by anything and asked him to examine it. However, a member of the surgeon's staff was confronted by the robed figure and was so shocked that, staggering back, she fell and broke a bone in her leg. Was this a message to the Setons who had a 'broken bone' as a display trophy? The surgeon returned the bone refusing to have anything more to do with it. This event suggests that whatever was the origin of the 'curse' it was linked to the bone itself and its removal from its rightful place of burial.

Back with Sir Alexander, the bone continued its baleful effect. Glasses and ornaments were found smashed on the floor the following morning. The events had a definite wearing effect on Sir Alexander who told the *Daily Express* in March 1937:

I can't explain these things. I wish I could for my own peace of mind. I laughed at the idea at first, but now I frankly confess that I am a little scared of the thing. I would willingly give the bone to anyone who would promise to treat it with respect. I will not have it destroyed, and I don't think it should be regarded as a joke and made a sort of party game.

In spite of all this Lady Seton had no intention of parting with the bone, believing that her illnesses had nothing to do with it as she had protected it and brought it from Egypt. However, according to later reports a priest was called in to exorcise the house. This did not seem to work so the bone was burnt and the ashes scattered. Then, apparently, the curse, if it was such, finally stopped. Or perhaps there had been some strange power in the bone which attracted, or activated, the poltergeist which was itself then destroyed as the bone finally burnt to nothing. Or, again, maybe the poltergeist simply moved on to carry out weird tricks elsewhere.

In 1954, Michael Rodgers made a strange claim from his home in Saughton. He reported that writing had been appearing on his sitting room walls since his wife had died a few years previously. What was even stranger was that Mr Rodgers claimed that the messages that were appearing could help solve the disappearance of Ian Aitken who, at that time, had been missing from his Edinburgh home for over two years. Mr Rogers explained that one night he had noticed that a street lamp shining through his front windows cast a pattern on the opposite wall. He believed that the pattern formed a 'three-quarter view' of his wife's face. Below it was another face which he believed to be that of a relative who died shortly after his wife. According to Mr Rogers, it was in fact the curtains which were the conduit for the effect, projection the supernatural image on the wall.

But, according to Mr Rogers, not only were faces appearing, but writing too. And it is this phenomenon which suggests that we are dealing here with a poltergeist. This writing, he believed, was an attempt by his wife to help solve a missing person case, that of ten-year-old Ian Aitken. Ian left his home at Newport Street on the afternoon of 3 September 1951, and simply disappeared. A journalist who visited the house reported that he could not make out the writing nor the faces described by Mr Rodgers and that what was being seen could have been a distortion of the street light as it passed through the window panes and lace curtains. That appears, on the face of it, a reasonable explanation. However, on the other hand, there is no doubt that dozens of people did see the images claimed by Michael Rogers, though whether it was truly his wife who was communicating with him must be open to doubt.

In the 1930s and 1940s, the then Edinburgh Psychic College had a 'Committee for the Recording of Abnormal Happenings'. Its members investigated and reported on alleged cases of haunting and poltergeist activity. One of its most sensitive cases involved poltergeist incidents at a city manse, the exact location of which has been kept under wraps up to the present day. The disturbances in the building had been of a very violent character. Furniture had been badly damaged and paintings on the walls would be found in the morning lying on the floor with their glass panes smashed to pieces. Several witnesses observed furniture not only moving by itself, but being thrown about with such force that if people had been hit they would have certainly been injured. Curtains spontaneously caught fire when it was clear that there was no one present. An exorcism carried out did nothing to stop the incidents. One member of the committee who visited the manse reported that after she had left the sitting room she heard a crash. She immediately rushed back in to find that a table in the room had been over-turned and the articles which had been lying on it were scattered across the floor. She was sure that no one could have passed her to get into the room. It was undoubtedly good first-hand evidence that 'something' was causing these strange events to occur. It seems, however, that the number of incidents became less frequent and then died out. And that, generally, is the only assurance that can be given to those who find themselves victims of the 'noisy spirit'. Experience shows that no matter how intensive the level of activity it normally passes over in time though no one can be sure why.

In the early years of the new millennium, I was called in to investigate a strange series of events that had occurred in premises in the Barnton area. The house, which occupied two floors, was an old building with modern additions. Ann, who had moved in with her children, had sensed soon after they arrived that the building was generating an unhappy atmosphere. She wasn't wrong. Ann had only been there a few months when a series of inexplicable events took place.

Ann was working in the kitchen one evening when she heard the sound of glass breaking and then crashing against the wall. It seemed to come from the sitting room which faced on to the back garden. Ann ran through just in time to see a foot pulling back through the smashed pane. Bravely she went over to take a look, but there was no one to be seen. She sensed though did not immediately fully appreciate that there was something odd about the incident as she could not remember seeing a body attached to the leg, though the leg had appeared solid enough. That thought, however, occurred later. In the meantime, she ran upstairs and looked out, but there appeared to be no one about. She called the police. They conducted an immediate search of the garden, but there was no sign of any intruder and, what was puzzling, no evidence of the footprints the police might have expected to find. It was all rather odd.

The following day, an equally strange incident took place. At around 9 a.m. Ann's young daughter told her that there was a strange man dressed all in black staring through the glass in the door. When Ann opened it there was no one there, but there was blood on parts of the woodwork. Disturbed, especially after the previous night's events, Ann called the police. A search was made of the house and though nothing had been stolen they discovered splashes of blood, several quite substantial, in Ann's bedroom, but nowhere else. It was bizarre and even the police could not explain it. How had someone entered the premises, bled all over one small area of the house, and then disappeared without being seen?

A few months later, Ann was lying in bed asleep when she suddenly woke up feeling completely paralysed. She felt as if someone or something was lying across her chest. As she watched the handset of the phone at the bedside lifted itself from its resting place, shot over and crashed against her head. Then she saw the outline of a tall, dark figure moving around the room. The whole experience felt unreal and passed as quickly as it had come on. As Ann recovered from her shock she began to wonder whether it had been some strange dream. She walked over to a mirror and stepped back in shock. There on her forehead was a large bruise exactly where the handset had caught her. It had certainly not been a dream. But what on earth was going on?

Ann became aware of more strange incidents. The sound of footsteps, heavy and confident, walking up and down the hall could often be heard. The bedroom door would swing open, but there would be no one there. One weekend, at around 12.30 in the morning, Ann was watching a film. During the break she headed for the toilet and on the way she heard a wailing voice which she thought was coming from one of the bedrooms. She stood outside listening. The sounds seemed definitely to be originating from inside. It sounded like someone in distress. However, when she summoned up the courage to go into the room it was empty and the sound now seemed to be coming from outside the front door. Ann went to take a look, but again there was no one there. The moans continued, however, sounding increasingly like someone in pain. It was definitely the voice of a woman. The sounds were upsetting and being unable to locate the source was, as Ann told me, frightening. So much so that she decided to, as she put it, 'barricade ourselves in my bedroom' where she remained till it was light.

It's often reported that animals seem aware of a presence even more so than their owners. Ann's dog would bark and growl in the direction of the living room door even when there was no one there. When the wailing incident happened he hid under the bed and wouldn't come out. At other times he would stare at one corner of the living room and howl.

One evening, a few months later, Ann had several people in the house. They all heard the back door open and then a peculiar scratching noise. A friend went to the kitchen to investigate. There was a man standing there scratching the radiator. He was in his early twenties with distinctively red hair, dressed in a shirt and jeans. She was struck by the fact that he was very pale, almost ghostly looking. She ran back to tell the others, but when they all went through there was no one there. Only a few seconds had passed, but the man had simply disappeared. No one had heard the door shut, but when they tried it was not only closed, but locked just as Ann knew she always left it. Had this been a poltergeist entity in human form?

These events were certainly unusual both in the length of time they continued and their intensity and variety. They showed no signs of simply stopping and may have been the exception to the rule that the phenomenon lasts for only a short period and gradually fades away. There are, however, some investigators, and I include myself, who doubt that we can simply slot unexplained phenomena into convenient, exclusive pigeonholes. Poltergeist and ghost activity often appear to overlap and other weird entities too may be a part of some strange 'other world', which we are simply unable to understand.

3

Witchcraft, Magic and Satanism

In the 1980s, the leading paranormal expert of his day, Edinburgh's Charles Cameron, commented: 'There is no doubt that the Lothians has more than its fair share of ghosts and weird happenings. This could be due to the large number of witches' covens which operated in the area.' What Charles Cameron was suggesting was that the activities of covens in and around the city over the centuries, the acts of ritual magic they had engaged in, and psychic warfare between individual witches, had a deep influence. By constantly disturbing the ether, witch covens had allowed spirits, poltergeists and other entities easy access to our dimension and this could explain why Edinburgh was such a hot spot of paranormal activity.

But if Charles Cameron was right, how had such a situation come about? Witchcraft in the Lothians has a long pedigree, but exactly how it developed remains a mystery. Druids and other pagan sects were active and many of the practices carried out by witches appear to be based on ancient pagan rites. Certainly the spells and potions allegedly used by witches seem to have been passed down the centuries and were used in rituals carried out for a variety of reasons, from curing illness to catching criminals. But why were these acts of magic suddenly seen as threatening? And why did those who used ritual magic become branded as witches almost overnight? Is it possible that a supernatural entity who we call the Devil emerged from another dimension and began to use selected individuals to create disorder? Witchcraft may be branded as 'fantasy', but those who claimed to have met Satan had no doubt that they were encountering an entity of some kind. And those at the receiving end of witchcraft believed in the supernatural powers of witches. People feared that a secret army of evildoers existed, which was engaged in a deadly war against mankind, and that their commander-in-chief was the Devil himself.

And if King James VI sitting in Holyrood Palace with his court of sophisticated nobles could take the threat from witchcraft seriously, is it any wonder that his subjects felt they had even more reason to be afraid? James was brought up in an atmosphere where the activities of witches were seen as part and parcel of the landscape. In 1479, the Earl of Mar was accused of trying to kill his brother King James III by witchcraft and, in 1537, Lady Glamis was burned alive for using magic charms against King James V. In fact James VI considered the power of witchcraft so dangerous that he wrote a book exposing and condemning their practices. It was called *Demonology*. James had good reason to be nervous. He believed he had been targeted by a coven of witches who had used various spells in an attempt to murder him. This conspiracy to kill the king by black magic even involved one of the leading noblemen of the time, the Earl of Bothwell.

The bizarre events of 1590, which have been seen by many to prove that witchcraft was a reality, started in an innocent manner. Gillie Duncan, a servant and general help, apparently developed overnight an ability to cure the sick and she was often consulted for remedies when people fell ill. But not everyone found this so comforting. Suspicions were aroused, especially those of her employer David Seaton. He was convinced that Gillie's ability to heal must have come from some other-worldly source and, to prove it, he had her tortured to get to the truth. Gillie's fingers were squeezed in thumbscrews and her head and neck wrenched with a knotted rope. She refused, however, to confess to any wrongdoing so Seaton stripped her naked and searched her body for evidence of a mark left by the Devil; a 'seal' that Satan was believed to put on his followers to brand them like cattle to show that they now belonged to him. Seaton claimed that he found just such a mark on Gillie's neck. Gillie was put in gaol where she underwent further torture in an effort to force a confession from her.

Gillie, in fact, did confess. So had Seaton been right all along? She alleged that several of her neighbours had sold their souls to Satan, including Agnes Sampson, known as 'the wise woman of Keith', Robert Grierson, a sailor, 'the potter's wife at Seaton', and 'the smith at the Briggs Hall'. Those she named were certainly no' big fish', though Agnes Sampson was destined to play a key role as events unfolded, but the ears of the witch-hunters pricked up when Gillie mentioned Dr John Fian as one of Satan's followers. The investigation immediately took a sharp turn, one that ended right at the heart of the Scottish Government.

John Fian was, on the face of it, a simple country school teacher who lived at Saltpans near Tranent. His job seemed far removed from the world of political machination, but Fian also acted as secretary to the Earl of Bothwell, a descendant of the husband of Mary Queen of Scots. What set minds racing, when Fian was accused of witchcraft, was that Bothwell was suspected by the king of planning to overthrow him and take the crown for himself. There had not always been bad blood between them. James had at one time trusted the Earl to such an extent that, when he sailed to Denmark to take home his bride-to-be, Anne of Denmark, he left Bothwell in charge of the country. However, on his return he heard rumours, which he apparently took seriously, that Bothwell had used the time the king was abroad to build up a power base which he intended to use to make himself king. James, always fearful and distrusting, was certainly at this time looking for an opportunity to bring Bothwell down. If the Earl was implicated in witchcraft then the Devil had, however unwittingly, provided James with the chance to deal with this formidable, though earthly, enemy, and strike a blow against Satan at the same time.

And not only did Bothwell have a close association with Fian, it was also claimed that he visited Agnes Sampson regularly who was well known in the area as a healer and white witch, and had asked her to predict the date of the king's death. To predict the monarch's life span by means of magic was treason and those found guilty could face execution. Bothwell, however, was too powerful simply to be treated in the way Gillie Duncan had been. James was determined though and personally interviewed Agnes Sampson, ordering that she be returned to prison and a confession forced from her when she refused to admit to being a witch.

As a suspected witch, Agnes was immediately tortured. Her neck was twisted by the use of a knotted rope and the 'witches bridle', an iron head cage with four sharp prongs, forced into her mouth. When this didn't bring an admission of guilt she was beaten about the head, stripped naked, shaved of all hair until at last the Devil's mark was found, a discoloured patch around her genitals. Faced with this evidence Agnes confessed that she belonged to a coven of witches who had been plotting to murder King James by witchcraft. She was taken to Holyrood Palace so that James could hear the details straight from Agnes's mouth, and a truly bizarre story emerged.

Agnes explained that the coven to which she belonged met at North Berwick Kirk and it was here that they had gathered on All Hallow's Eve while James was in Denmark to meet Anne, his bride-to-be. Their intention at this time was to create a magic spell to kill James. They formed a circle, holding hands and performed a reel, chanting words of magic while Gillie Duncan provided the music on a harp. At a signal the reel came to a sudden halt and the coven, led by Gillie, moved in procession to the kirk. Candles were burning on the altar and flames turning blue signalled the arrival of the Devil himself who appeared as an ordinary man dressed in dark clothes. He now ordered the members of the coven to submit to him and, stretching himself naked across the altar, ordered each witch to kiss his bare buttocks.

James was doubtful about Agnes's account, but Gillie Duncan was brought in. She confirmed the details given by Agnes even to the extent of playing the tune on a harp she had played at North Berwick Kirk. Was this independent confirmation that these events had really happened? Agnes then told James that from the pulpit the Devil had branded the king as 'the greatest enemy I have in the world'. She added to the mix more strange tales of travel by magic to distant lands, the recruitment of an army of witches and plots hatched to murder and maim.

James had had enough. 'You are all liars', he barked. Now came a bizarre turning point. Agnes approached James and whispered in his ear the very words that had passed between him and Queen Anne in their bedroom suite on the very first night of their marriage. 'By the living gods', James retorted in amazement, 'all the Devils in Hell could not have discovered the same'. In a second he was convinced that some kind of black magic had been used to eavesdrop on this private conversation. It was a simple moment that was to have severe repercussions.

So why did Agnes do it? And how did she know what James had said to Anne? We do not know what words were spoken so it is hard to be sure if Agnes could have simply guessed. But she was taking a risk even in claiming the knowledge as if she was wrong then she would immediately be discredited. But, it has to be asked, why would she want to be proved right? Because in doing so she branded herself by her own mouth as a witch with the inevitable result of being involved in a plot to murder the king. And there could be no escape from an inevitable fate.

The noose connecting the Earl of Bothwell, Agnes Sampson and John Fian was being drawn tighter. Agnes claimed that Fian had asked to carry a letter to another member of the coven, arranging a date to carry out a black magic ceremony on the shore of the Firth of Forth. This may have been the plan to whip up a storm with the Devil's help intended to sink the King's boat as it sailed back from Denmark. However, Agnes claimed that even before this attempt she had been plotting to kill James by witchcraft.

She trapped a black toad, hung it up by its heels from the branch of a living tree for three days and collected the venom as it dropped. There are no black toads in Scotland and none that are venomous so it would seem likely that Agnes meant that a magic spell or ritual was used to turn fluid from the toad into poison. But how could Agnes Sampson possibly get close enough to James to administer the venom? The mystery undoubtedly deepens and the way she achieved this suggests, at the very least, some strange goings on. By some manner she got in touch with, or perhaps knew, James Kerr, an attendant in the King's bedchamber. He had access to James's clothes. Agnes asked him to rub the poison on one of James's shirts. If he couldn't manage that Kerr was to cut a piece of any article which James wore next to his body and pass it to her. She would rub the poison into it and through magic it would kill the king. Kerr would have nothing to do with it, but didn't report Agnes's approach to James. It's odd that there is no evidence that he was ever pulled up or questioned over the matter. One more puzzling issue within these enigmatic events.

It may have been the failure of Agnes's plan that led to the coven, on John Fian's orders, gathering at the Water of Leith where it emptied into the Forth. A cat caught that day was christened with James's name and, for the purpose of the act of magic, became James. The arms and legs of a corpse had been obtained and were tied to the animal. The coven then sailed out to sea and, chanting in a ritual manner, threw the cat with the limbs attached into the water. They watched and continued chanting as the creature drowned. It died as the coven believed James would now die; the victim of the storm they believed they had conjured up through their magic. And a storm did, in fact, erupt and sank a ship sailing out to meet the King's convoy as it arrived in the Forth. The ship that the king was aboard was saved from the storm because, as Agnes explained, 'his great Christian faith blunted our evil and brought him safely to shore.'

Agnes's confession was not good news for the Earl of Bothwell who, growing increasingly nervous over the turn of events, retreated to Crichton Castle in East Lothian and waited to see what would happen next. The taint of 'witchcraft' grew increasingly close as his secretary John Fian was taken into custody.

John Fian was not the Tranent schoolmaster's real name. It was, in fact, John Cunningham and the designation 'Dr Fian' must have been a nickname of some kind revealing the view of people at the time of his activities. 'Fian' is clearly derived from *Fean, Feane* or *Fianne,* all of which refer to a 'fairy' or other-world connection. Cunningham was seen as either a man with second sight or a man who dabbled in those areas which lay beyond the power of ordinary men.

Following his arrest Fian was given the chance to confess, but denied being a witch or part of a coven. However, the authorities were determined to get him to admit his guilt. The gaolers clamped the apparatus known as the 'Spanish boot' to each of his legs. This encased the area from the knee to the shin in metal. It prevented the bone from breaking immediately as an iron hammer was crashed repeatedly against the 'boot', but the pain was terrible and the legs of the victim were soon reduced to a bruised and battered pulp. Fian still didn't confess even though the pain made him lose consciousness.

There was little pity. The fact that he had survived this brutal torture was seen simply as more proof of his guilt. It seemed unnatural that any human being could withstand such violence. It may have been Agnes Sampson or Gillie Duncan who suggested that Fian had cast a spell of his own and advised his mouth be examined. When the gaolers did as Agnes advised they found two pins pushed into the roof of his mouth. These had been inserted by Fian himself, it was believed, as a magic rite so that his senses would be numb to the pain being inflicted on his body. Remarkably, when the pins were removed Fian's resolve evaporated and in front of the King he wrote a confession of his involvement with the North Berwick coven. It turned out that Fian was a key member of the coven and was held in high regard by Satan who appointed him as his secretary. He recorded the coven membership, issued oaths of obedience and passed on the Devil's orders to his followers. He sat next to his master and walked beside him in their ritual ceremony, anti-clockwise around the kirk graveyard, an act intended to cleanse the cemetery of its Christian sanctity. The fact that, as well as acting as secretary to the Devil, Fian held the same position with the Earl of Bothwell could hardly have escaped general

notice. The implication was obvious. Indeed it was suggested
that the Earl of Bothwell himself might be the figure who stood
in the pulpit at North Berwick kirk and was the leader of the
witches coven. It's a view that has found favour among some
right down to today.

Fian described how Satan had led the coven into the graveyard and, standing over a grave, bent a hand towards the ground
which opened slowly by itself to reveal a fresh corpse. At a
signal from the Devil the women among the coven pulled the
body from its grave and hacked off the arms and legs. It was
these limbs which were later used in the ceremony at Leith to
sink the king's ship.

Fian was placed in solitary confinement where events took
place that were so strange that it raises questions of just exactly
what transpired. Fian, it was reported, talked of 'renouncing
the Devil and all his works' and vowed to 'lead the life of a
Christian'. He claimed that Satan had come to him in his cell
during the night, dressed in black and carrying a white wand
as a symbol of his authority. The Devil challenged Fian to keep
faith with him 'according to your first oath and promise' and
asked him to continue to be his follower as he was his most
trusted servant. Fian, however, had had enough and retorted,
'I have listened to you too much and because of this you have
brought me down. I utterly forsake you!' Satan's chilling reply
would surely have struck terror into any man's heart. 'Once you
die', Satan informed him coldly, 'you shall be mine.' Did Fian
invent this conversation? Did he imagine it? Or was he, in fact,
in communication with an entity from some realm outside this
world? Fian himself appeared convinced that he was in thrall
to some supernatural being. Should we doubt him?

Fian faced certain death, but who attempted to save him?
During the night a key was passed into his cell and he not only
walked from it without being seen but passed through the whole

of Edinburgh Castle. His amazing escape was put down to the work of the Devil and if it was down to straightforward bribes no one seems to have been punished for it. But if human help was behind it who would risk involvement as they would immediately be tarred with the witchcraft brush? And Fian himself seems to have adopted a bizarre route once free. Instead of making himself scarce he headed straight back to Saltpans, an area where he could hardly escape being recognised. So why did he go there? Had he been freed to pass on a message? Was he on a mission to destroy incriminating evidence? Was he let out to perform a magic ritual of some kind? Or was it a trick to see if he would head for Crichton Castle?

The last seems unlikely as Fian was quickly recaptured, discovered, so it was said, in his own home, sitting at the table apparently unconcerned as to his fate. His attitude had changed dramatically which suggests that something had happened in the hours since he had escaped. He now denied any involvement with witchcraft and denounced his confession. Why he adopted this stance raises many questions. He had already admitted being a witch and so there was no chance he would escape a death sentence, and he must have known that he would face torture again to force him to confess. Back in prison he was chained to the ground while his nails were pulled from his fingers and sharp needles driven into the exposed flesh. His legs which had not healed from the previous battering, were put once more inside the Spanish boot and hit with a hammer. As the records state, 'his legs were crushed and beaten together, as small as might be, and the bones and flesh so bruised that the blood and marrow spouted forth in great abundance. They were unserviceable forever.' But, incredibly, John Fian still refused to confess. However, as he had admitted guilt earlier James believed that he could go on trial and an inevitable guilty verdict followed. On 13 January 1591, unable to walk, Fian was carried in a cart and strangled to death before his body was burnt.

At this point, it was certainly dangerous to have been too closely linked to Bothwell. Euphemia McLean was a known associate of the Earl and had been named by Gillie Duncan as one of the coven members. Evidence was presented that Euphemia had asked Agnes Sampson to help her to murder her father-in-law, John Moscrop. Agnes, for her part, had been charged with 'making a wax figure of John Mocsrop, father-in-law to Euphemia McLean, at Euphemia's request, for the destruction of John Moscrop.' Agnes had taken the wax figure to a hill where by magic ritual she 'raised the Devil', who using his supernatural powers 'confirmed the picture to serve for the destruction of John Moscrop.' Having completed the ritual, Agnes delivered the wax image to Janet Drummond, servant to Euphemia, telling her to put it under John Moscrop's bed. By black magic, Satan had imbued the figure with the ability to suck the life force from Moscrop and take it into itself. The wax figure could then be destroyed and its destruction would bring about Moscrop's death. Here was the Devil, his followers, black magic ritual and murder all neatly brought together. The jury, however, refused to convict, but changed their mind after James threatened them. Euphemia was burnt alive.

Bothwell had already been arrested on 15 April 1591, and put in the castle gaol. To add to his problems, Ritchie Gordon, well known as a devotee of black magic, who had been burned to death at Edinburgh Cross in February, had confessed to preparing spells to kill the king at the request of the Earl. There seemed to be a pattern established. Bothwell was associating with known sorcerers with the aim of murdering James. The Earl denied it all, of course, but not trusting to justice escaped from the castle and managed to avoid all attempts at recapturing him. Interestingly, in a statement he issued denying any treasonable activities, he admitted associating with Ritchie Gordon and claimed that Ritchie, Sampson and Fian had been put to death because they had recanted their confession. In other words, he was the victim of a plot rather than the king. Bothwell clearly had allies and James was not able to act against him though he did not return to court till 1593. Was he, as some suspect, at the heart of a wider network of witches? James was so convinced of the reality of the Devil and his covens as a result of these events that he wrote his *Demonology*, published in 1597, arguing that 'the assaults of Satan are most certainly practised and his servants [that is, witches] therefore merit most severely to be punished.' Writers up to the present have been convinced that Bothwell was the 'High Priest' of an ancient religion and that he did indeed organise his followers into covens. His 'witches' went to their death while other coven leaders, individuals of high position, escaped and carried on practising in secret.

Bothwell's status may have saved him from James's wrath, but the Earl may have suffered from the past reputation of his family, especially that of his uncle, James, Earl of Bothwell, who had married Mary Queen of Scots. He too had a reputation as a witch and it was alleged that he had used magic spells to induce Mary to fall in love with him. Certainly, it is generally agreed that her infatuation with him bordered on the suicidal, and her marriage to him sealed her fate, sparking a rebellion which forced her to abandon her throne and leave Scotland forever. In fact, witchcraft was seen as a tool of the upper classes as they battled for control of Scotland. Janet Beaton, Lady Buccleuch, not only a friend but a mistress of Bothwell, was suspected of using witchcraft to help the Earl to take advantage of Mary. The Earl of Leslie and the Earl of Lennox, aristocratic 'powerbrokers' and advisers to the Crown both accused Bothwell of using secret magic rites in order to influence people. It was believed that Bothwell's interest in black magic had been stimulated during the period that he was educated in France where, it was said, he spent most of his time reading up on sorcery and magic. It was alleged that Janet Beaton had the power to conjure up spirits and the ability to make them do what she wanted. A dangerous and double-edged weapon, as any true magician would warn the novice. But she survived it all, though her husbands were less fortunate. She went through four and married a fifth at the age of sixty-one. She seemed a timeless beauty which, of course, raised questions of just how she managed to keep her good looks. But Queen Mary herself was not free of the suspicion of using black magic. Margaret, Lady Atholl, one of her ladies-in-waiting , was spoken of openly as a woman who had studied magic with an expert — exactly with whom is unclear — and when Mary was giving birth to the future James VI had transferred, by ritual means, the pains Mary was experiencing to one of her helpers, the unfortunate Lady Reres.

Mary Queen of Scots would surely have advised her son, the future James VI, to be wary of secret covens of witches. She had direct experience of their work. Lord Ruthven, a leading noble during Mary's reign, was suspected of being a warlock who regularly cast spells, though he used more direct tactics in murdering Rizzio, Mary's Italian favourite. It was he who organised and led the band of killers into Mary's apartment at Holyrood and took the lead in stabbing Rizzio to death right in front of her. Henry, Lord Darnley, Mary's young husband, was certainly involved in the plot though he took no direct part in Rizzio's death. It was because of this incident that Mary fell out with Darnley leading people to suspect that she planned his death in revenge. Black magic, of course, was believed to have been involved in this equally notorious, and still unsolved, murder.

The facts are simple. On the night of Sunday, 9 February 1567, while Henry, Lord Darnley lay ill at Kirk O'Field House, situated near South Bridge where the University now stands, a massive explosion took place which blew the building apart. Shortly afterwards Darnley was found dead in the grounds outside the house. His body did not have the appearance of someone who had been killed in an explosion. It looked as if he had been strangled and his body dumped outside. Why then had there been an attempt to blow up the house? Was it a ruse to conceal the murder? And was Mary involved?

The argument rages on to this day. There were some inexplicable aspects. How had it been possible to smuggle into the building which was by no means a large one, the many casks of gunpowder that would be needed to blow Kirk O'Field sky high? It wasn't as if Darnley was alone, he had a whole retinue of servants, and the commotion made by bringing in a large pile of heavy gunpowder barrels could hardly have passed unnoticed. But somehow it had been done. Those in the know did, of course, have an answer. Bothwell had connived with the Queen to dispatch her unstable husband and he had used black magic to carry out the murder. Janet Beaton with her power over entities from other worlds had the gunpowder brought in silently. To make sure, however, Darnley had been killed separately by invisible fiends so that no one heard a sound.

After these epic sixteenth-century struggles between good and evil, which went to the very heart of upper-class society, why did witchcraft simply fade away? At the highest levels people stopped accusing each other of being members of a coven. But elsewhere witches appear to have been as active as ever. The life of Agnes Fynnie, who was charged with witchcraft in 1644, is a fascinating insight into the phenomenon of black magic at street level. Agnes, who lived in Potter Row, was suspected by her neighbours of using her dark powers to revenge herself on those who dared to cross her path. The young son of her neighbour, William Fairlie, passed by Agnes and made a comment to her. She was offended and made no secret of the fact. Soon after the boy became paralysed down his left side, was bedridden and quickly wasted away, dying within a week. The doctors who attended found that they could do nothing to help the lad and claimed that he had died because of some inexplicable supernatural event. Another neighbour, Beatrice Nisbet, was struck dumb, an affliction she attributed to Agnes's powers of witchcraft. Janet Grinton, a trader in fish, also fell foul of Agnes after she sold the 'witch' a pair of herring that Agnes believed were not fresh. She took the fish back and demanded her money be returned, warning Janet that she would die soon. Shortly after Janet died as Agnes had predicted. The evidence against Agnes was mounting.

However, though people were afraid of Agnes's powers, they also turned to her for help. John Buchan's son was suffering from some kind of paralysis known at the time as 'palsy'. Agnes visited the child advising the parents to leave the room and pray for the health of their son. However, when they returned they found their son's condition had worsened dramatically and his paralysis was so bad that he was unable to move any part of his body. A large wound had appeared at the top of his right thigh which was 'as wide as the palm of a hand as if a large chunk of meat had been hacked out of it.' Was it believed that Agnes herself had done this? Even eaten it? Or had the Devil himself attacked the child? That may defy belief, but Agnes, faced with the parents' suspicions, threatened, in retaliation, to summon up the Devil to take a bite out of Buchan's wife. A week later the child died.

John Buchan accused Agnes of being a witch and threatened to pay her back for the death of his child. It was a rash if understandable act. That night he became ill and had a high fever but by the next day felt better; well enough in fact to warn Agnes that he intended to spread the news of her witching of his family round the whole town, unless she lifted the spell she had cast against them. As if by magic Buchan's illness departed, but he eventually died of a mysterious complaint after falling out with Agnes again. The odd thing is that Buchan's wife had been trying to buy a cake from Agnes on credit and was refused. This led to an argument. It was this dispute which led Agnes to cast a death spell on John Buchan in reprisal.

Agnes fell out with many individuals who soon after suffered some strange misfortune. Euphemia Kincaid argued with Agnes and called her a 'witch.' Agnes replied, coolly, that if this was the case then Euphemia's family had better be careful. Soon after a wooden beam fell on Euphemia's daughter and broke her leg. No one was safe from Agnes's devilish power, it seemed.

She was even prepared to defy the law. Robert Watt, head of the Shoemaker's union and a local magistrate, fined Agnes's son-in-law John Purves for a breach of the peace. On hearing the news an enraged Agnes walked over to where the shoemakers were holding a meeting and hit Watt over the head. Was what happened next simply coincidence? Robert Watt's business went into decline and nothing he could do seemed able to halt it. One day Agnes turned up at Robert's house and reminded him bluntly of her assault. She warned him if he did not make up with her and her son-in-law his business would go bankrupt. Robert Watt threw in the towel and returned the fine John had been forced to pay. He also apologised. After that Watt's business became as prosperous as before. No one saw that as pure chance.

The odd thing is that Agnes herself ran a general store of some kind and, in spite of her reputation, people seem to have used it so must have been aware of the risk they were taking.

One of her customers, Christine Harlow, having ordered salt returned it with a message to Agnes that the amount she had received was far less than she'd paid for. Shortly after, Christine was taken ill. It seemed as if she would die so Agnes was sent for. The view was that Christine recovered after Agnes's visit because 'the witch had lifted the spell she had put on her.'

Her neighbours grew increasingly afraid of Agnes. John Cockburn fell out with Agnes's daughter and was terrified when Agnes appeared in his bedroom one night. She had got into the house even though the windows and doors were bolted. There's no evidence that Agnes took any action against him but such a supernatural appearance was enough to convince him that he was dealing with a witch. Margaret Williamson crossed Agnes and in reply Agnes openly called on the Devil to 'blow her blind.' Soon after Margaret became ill and lost the power of sight.

Faced with these displays of black magic the authorities must have felt they had little choice. Agnes was accused of having consulted with, and of having been, a follower of Satan for nearly thirty years. It was also claimed that she had herself boasted of being no 'ordinary' witch but a 'grand, proud and noble' witch. The evidence could hardly be denied and Agnes was strangled to death and her body burnt to ashes. Agnes' life raises many questions. She clearly believed herself to possess strange powers. But was she deluded or did she, in fact, belong to some kind of strange cult? And was she really in touch with the Devil? Those who lived with her did not doubt it, nor did they dispute her supernatural abilities which she used for both good and evil.

Witchcraft has always been a double-edged sword, but in some cases there appears little good about it. When considering the events surrounding the case of Thomas Weir several key questions come to mind. Does his confession suggest that there was indeed a network of witches active in seventeenth-century Edinburgh? If there was a 'Devil' then just exactly what was he up to? But do some of the details admitted to by Weir suggest that we are dealing with an altogether more complex and radically different scenario?

Weir was an unlikely witch. He'd been a soldier and fought in the English Civil War in Ireland, on behalf of Parliament against Charles I. He appeared to be a committed Puritan and was believed to be so true to the faith that he was one of those appointed to guard the arch royalist John Graham, Marquis of Montrose, when he was executed in the capital in May 1650. Weir went down in history as the man who notoriously blew pipe smoke in John Graham's face as he went to the scaffold. But history was to be kinder to John Graham than Thomas Weir as events were to show. Weir, however, was held in high esteem and became Captain of the Edinburgh City Guard. He also took up preaching and earned a reputation as a devout man who visited the homes of leading men of the city to pray alone with their wives. No one had a bad word to say about him or any suspicion that Weir was not what he appeared to be. And he might have carried on with his bizarre double life if, for unknown reasons, he had not suddenly experienced a crisis of conscience. Or so he claimed.

Out of the blue in front of a group of friends he blurted out that for fifty years he had been a servant of Satan. But he did not stop there and began detailing, to anyone who would listen, a shocking and sordid story. He confessed not only to having regular sex with his sister, Grizelle, with whom he admitted he had lived as man and wife, but also with the wives and daughters of leading city members; the ones the trusting men folk had willingly allowed Weir to visit to give spiritual comfort. Many of the men involved were personal friends of his.

And he also claimed to have visited several women in the

middle of the night. He had managed to gain secret entry to their bedrooms through occult powers given to him by his master the Devil. Weir confessed that Satan had given him a magic staff which not only made him invisible, but enabled him to get inside people's houses. In this manner, he had made his way into the houses of women he knew and had sex with them while their husbands slept by their side. It seemed an outrageous claim and people at first were disbelieving. It was also not clear whether or not the women involved had been active participants in these sexual encounters or whether they were put into some kind of trance and were unaware of Weir's presence. No women would admit to voluntary sex with Weir but the thought that he'd engaged in such activity without his victim being aware of it was disturbing and frightening. Even more bizarre was Weir's claim that he had engaged in sexual intercourse with a horse in a farmer's field. The man's sanity was doubted and his confessions were ignored. The general hope was that he would somehow come to his senses and events would blow over.

But the opposite happened. Weir insisted that what he admitted was absolutely true. To the perceptive it began to dawn that perhaps Weir was sending out a warning, alerting people to the entity which he now felt he had allowed to control, and ruin, his life. But as Weir kept talking it was realised that the only solution, as it was growing into a city scandal, was to lock him in the Tolbooth and charge him with witchcraft.

This only served to increase Weir's self-denunciation. And worse was to follow. Grizelle Weir, his sister, now came forward to back up Thomas's story. She confirmed that they had both met with Satan, become his servants and engaged in the various sexual activities her brother had confessed to. The authorities were left with little choice. Both Thomas and Grizelle were put on trial. And here one more curious twist emerges. The charges of witchcraft against Weir were dropped and he was charged instead with 'incest, sodomy and bestiality.' He could hardly deny it. Found guilty he was executed, going willingly to his death. Grizelle, on the other hand, was executed on the grounds of having consulted with 'witches, necromancers and devils.'

Naturally, the different way in which Thomas was dealt with, compared to Grizelle, aroused suspicion. As Thomas had been the one to come forward and confess to being a witch why had he escaped that indictment? It was understandable that those with whom he had worked and been friendly with might not want to be tarred with the same brush. But was there more to it than that? Could there have been a coven involving several leading men of the city? It seemed a reasonable question, especially as rumours swept Edinburgh that Weir had been allowed to escape the gallows and a mental patient, a look-alike, had been substituted at the scaffold. Soon after, several witnesses claimed to have seen him walking the villages of the Lothians still grasping the stick gifted him by Satan.

So how much was simply the product of Weir's twisted mind? Sex with a horse seems at first to be the confession of a deranged mind. However, this strange act was part of an ancient pagan rite. The Kings of Ulster in ancient times ritually copulated with a mare to achieve long life. A horse was regarded as a sacred animal by ancient pagan cults and contact with a horse, and parts of a horse, as used in ritual magic are still seen today as bestowing certain psychic gifts. Most strange of all, however, is Weir's claim about how he travelled around the capital. According to him, the Devil possessed a 'flying chariot'. This was undoubtedly a nuts-and-bolts machine which spurted flame as it travelled across the skies. The Devil sent it to Weir to carry him to their meetings. And this happened, according to Weir, in broad daylight. This must rank as the most bizarre of all his strange admissions. A 'UFO' mixed up in witchcraft? Admittedly, it fails to make much sense and raises some very disturbing questions. But why would Weir invent such a story? Can we really accept that some alien entity set out deliberately to corrupt Weir and others? What would be the point of such an act? Maybe we have to admit that many of the actions of ghosts, poltergeists and other entities encountered in the city do seem to serve no purpose whatsoever. Maybe there simply isn't one.

Thomas Weir's revelations were the last great flurry of witchcraft in the city. Belief in the power of witches seemed to disappear and the acts against witchcraft were repealed in 1736. But it created another mystery. What happened to witchcraft between the ending of the witch trials and the twentieth century, when witchcraft underwent a revival and came out into the open? Some suggest that it never really disappeared. It just went underground. The suspicion is that, at the top of society, witchcraft was as thriving and as active as it had been at the time of King James VI. The upper classes simply kept quiet about their involvement in witch covens and, to make their activities even more secure, they ridiculed and got rid of laws against witchcraft. Now they could carry on their secret activities with no fear of prosecution. What re-emerged in the twentieth century was witchcraft at street level as the wider public began to rediscover ancient practices that were once part and parcel of daily life. It was not, however, without danger for the participants as our ancestors knew only too well. The dark side of the covens was about to be learnt all over again.

By the 1990s, witchcraft was thriving in the capital. It was claimed that there had been a rapid growth in the number of witches in Edinburgh, with nearly twenty active covens and for those involved it, no doubt, formed a harmless and even enjoyable new approach to living. But some found there was a less welcoming side.

Through my involvement in investigating the paranormal, I came into contact with several members of Wiccan covens. Most were at pains to explain the benefits and peaceful nature of modern witchcraft. I didn't for a moment doubt their sincerity. A few, however, had some distinctly strange tales to tell. Gordon had certainly experienced a series of bizarre incidents while a member of a city coven. He first called me in 2002 and we met a number of times in various cafés during which he told me of the time he spent as a coven member. Gordon, in fact, was no dyed-in-the-wool Wiccan. In fact, he had drifted into coven membership through his girlfriend who had a long-time interest in the subject. At first, Gordon found the experience of attending coven meetings stimulating and not at all threatening. Gatherings took place in individual houses and he found the ritual aspects intriguing and even enjoyable. He laughed:

> There was no animal sacrifice or naked women on altars. None of the stuff you see in the films. There was a 'priest' with a cloak and we chanted while he lit candles and carried out ritual movements just things like that. To be honest it seemed quite harmless. There was plenty of chat and it was all very friendly.'

But after a few months things started to change. Gordon explained:

> We started meeting out of doors in spots well away from the public. Now we were expected to take our clothes off and spells were worked up against certain things and then particular individuals. It all started getting very intense. There seemed to be rivalry between the coven I was in and another group of witches. I felt it was getting a bit nasty.

71

Gordon was to learn just how nasty it could be when he fell out with the coven leader and, at the same time, drifted away from his girlfriend. He said:

> I made some comments about not liking the way the coven was going and at the same time I was breaking up with my girlfriend. A member of the coven I'd got quite friendly with warned me to be careful, but I just laughed it off.

Within a couple of weeks Gordon began to wonder if he had been right to take it so lightly. He explained:

> As I was walking home from work to the flat I rented on the south side, one evening in late October, I glimpsed a shadowy figure which seemed to be darting in and out of doorways opposite me but slightly behind me. I thought it must be a trick of the light at first. But then it happened a few days later when I was coming back from town after a night out and I was following a different route. What I kept catching sight of was simply a dark, human-shaped figure, but it seemed to vanish as soon as I tried to look directly at it. It made me nervous and I put it down to imagination, but it happened several times after that. But the incident that really freaked me took place in my flat. I got up to go to the toilet during the night. As I walked along the hall I caught sight of the shadowy figure. This time it was quite clear in that I could see it was wearing a dark cloak down to the floor and the head was covered by a hood. But the really frightening thing was that I could see a face. It was a man's, very white and scowling. I admit I shrieked in terror and the figure vanished. I stayed up all night with the lights on.

Gordon did not know what to make of it but was sure it wasn't all in his mind. He said:

I contacted the coven member I'd been friendly with. I'll call him 'Atremis'. Atremis agreed to see me as long as I kept quiet about it. He was nervous too. He told me that the coven leader was angry with me for speaking out and abandoning the coven. He was sending his spirit phantom to warn me not to reveal anything about the coven and to make sure I kept in line. Atremis gave me advice about rituals to use to keep the spirit phantom out of my flat. I did what Atremis advised and I didn't see the shadowy figure in the flat again, but it didn't leave me completely for several weeks as I saw it on a number of occasions when I walked home. I can understand people thinking I'm a fantasist, but until these things happened I had no belief in the power of witchcraft. Now I'm not so sure. I've kept well away from the covens ever since.

Gordon's is certainly a strange story for twenty-first century Scotland and it may all be down to the power of suggestion. It's well known that if a person starts to believe in the power of magic, and Gordon may have done so without being conscious of it, then the mind can start to imagine that it is being threatened by all manner of things. Gordon may have worried about falling out with the coven and his mind did the rest. But witches themselves would have no doubt that Gordon could have been the victim of a psychic attack.

In the late 1990s I met Dougie, a High Priest of a 'White Wiccan' coven, deeply immersed in the rites and belief of what he saw as an ancient religion. He most definitely represented those in the Wiccan community who see their religion as beneficial both to the individual and society. But even Dougie was not free from risk. Opposed to Satanism he found himself on the wrong side of those still following the teachings of the 'Great Beast', the notorious Black Magician, Aleister Crowley. To show their displeasure these disciples of the dark side sent a warning in the form of a bizarre entity called a 'gollum'. A gollum is created by black magicians using soil from an ancient graveyard. By means of strange rituals the black magicians resurrect the outward form of a dead person, which is then imbued with the power of an evil spirit and sent to terrify those they believe need to be taught a lesson. Dougie had been the victim of just such an attack. He told me of the terrifying night he had spent crouched in a corner of his New Town flat with the gollum standing over him. It was only when the sun rose that the attack came to an end. Dougie had managed to defeat the power of the gollum by using his athame, a sacred knife consecrated by Wiccan ritual, to prevent the gollum sucking the life force from his body. It was certainly a warning bell and Dougie took note. He explained that to protect his flat he had to' ritually block all entry points to the building so evil spirits can't enter.'

In the 1980s, I was friendly with a leading Wiccan at a time when witchcraft was just re-emerging from the shadows. Barry gave me an interesting account of how Wiccan magic works. He told me:

> In Wicca we believe that spirit guides can, and do, assist us with all forms of magic to change someone's mind about something. For example, some person is refusing to sell a house to a Wiccan couple who have offered a fair price.

According to Barry the spirit people would work to change the mind of those refusing to sell, provided that those buying were being fair. That on its own does not appear threatening and those like Barry would only deal with the spirit people on the basis of avoiding harm. But what of those who would contact spirits and demons for less benign purposes and use them to carry out acts of revenge? There certainly seems to be two sides to witchcraft and Gordon and Dougie appear to have been the victims of a strange power that most people would steer well clear of.

Certainly times have changed. In October 2004 the Royal Navy officially allowed a non-commissioned officer from Edinburgh to call himself a Satanist and practise his rituals on-board ship. This followed what was called 'Scotland's first legal white witch wedding', a ceremony held in a vault in the Old Town in September 2004. There's no doubt that this reflected a growing attraction to 'alternative' religions. But is there more to it than that? The issue today, as it was in the time of James VI, concerns the extent to which witchcraft has gone right to the top of society. Are those who make the rules, enforce the laws, or run large institutions involved in black magic? Or even Satanism? These people are unlikely to step forward and admit to being members of a coven. And it has to be said that I have never seen any direct evidence of the involvement of any public figure. Rumours though persist and I have been given accounts of covens gathering on remote hill sites deep in the heart of the Pentlands, attended by those who could, but would rather not, be recognised. The ability to carry out acts, good or evil, by supernatural means attracts a certain type of individual, as it has always done. The prospect that one might be able to contact other entities, or even the Devil, and enter into realms other than our own seems for some an opportunity too good to miss. And, of course, unlike witches of old no one today faces the prospect of gaol or death for being a follower of the 'horned god'.

4

Blood Lust of the Undead

Did ever a capital city boast a more weird thoroughfare than
Edinburgh's Princes Street? Ghosts, fairies, UFOs, the Devil
and entities which defy description have all appeared along its
route. But can it really be the haunt of vampires? An event at
the turn of the twentieth century suggests that this most frightening of beings is no stranger to the city streets. The witness
to the bizarre incident was twenty-three-year-old Geoffrey
Anderson. He recalled:

> On 23 November, I was about to cross from the corner of Princes
> Street into Hanover Street. At the other corner, opposite a large
> shop, stood a horse and carriage. The horse was turned towards
> me and about twenty yards away. Suddenly from the gutter, where
> it falls into the drain, rose a vague black shape about four feet
> long and two and a half feet high, but without any visible legs. It
> was shaped like an hour-glass and moved like a huge caterpillar
> towards the horse, about fifteen feet off. The movement was very
> rapid. It sprang to the throat of the animal, clung there like a
> limpet for an instant and disappeared. The horse, in evident
> terror, reared violently straight up, throwing out his hoofs as if
> to strike something. A passer-by went to its head and I succeeded
> in quieting the terrified creature. The streets were brilliantly lit

with electric light and the shop windows rendered the illumina-
tion greater. I cannot account for the appearance. My mind was
occupied with simple everyday objects of no great moment.

The description of this strange beast, although different from
the flesh-and-blood being we would usually associate with a
vampire, does reveal one of the characteristic traits of this entity.
It went straight for the horse's neck, clearly seeking to draw
sustenance from the blood flowing there. Vampires, in any case,
can take on many forms and the ability of the vampire to change
shape is one of its hallmark traits.

Vampires, if they ever went away, have certainly made a
comeback in the twenty-first century with a host of television
appearances, such as in *Bufffy the Vampire Slayer*, and in films,
such as *New Moon* part of the *Twilight* saga. It all seems like
harmless thrills, but, inevitably, there is a darker side, and a
price to be paid.

In October 2003, twenty-two-year-old Allan Menzies claimed
that he had achieved his ambition of becoming a vampire
following his killing of Thomas McKendrick in Fauldhouse,
West Lothian. Menzies, obsessed with vampire films, told the
High Court in Edinburgh, where he was on trial for murder,
that he attacked Thomas McKendrick , aged twenty-one, after
he insulted one of the characters in the adult-rated film, *Queen
of the Damned*, a 2002 film adaption of a novel in Anne Rice's
Vampire Chronicles series. It was a film that fascinated Menzies
to such an extent that he had watched it over a hundred times.
A key character in the film is the female vampire 'Akasha',
played by the US singer Aaliyah. Menzies claimed that Akasha
regularly visited his bedroom at night and they passed the time
talking about the vampire world. It was during these 'chats',
that Menzies realised that he wished to become a vampire and
live with Akasha. When he confided his secret wish to her,

Akasha told him that he could only achieve immortality and become a real vampire if he killed someone.

Was Menzies waiting for an opportunity to turn Akasha's words into reality? It seems likely as what happened next could hardly be described as coincidence. According to Menzies, Thomas McKendrick made insulting remarks about Akasha, calling her a 'black bitch.' What really infuriated Menzies, however, was the fact that his beloved vampire was standing beside him at the time. In Menzies' eyes she was a real person who had been offended by Thomas's words. He demanded that Thomas apologise which he did, but saying to Menzies at the same time, 'You can't believe in vampires.' But Menzies really did and Thomas's words enraged him. Grabbing a hammer, he chased Thomas upstairs where he battered him about the head. Leaving his victim unable to move and probably dying, Menzies went downstairs and took out a knife and a cup from the kitchen. He then slashed Thomas Mckendrick's throat, catching the spurting blood with the cup. He then drank it, filled it again and drank a second time. But that was by no means the end of the bizarre and horrific series of events. Menzies claimed that he broke off and ate a portion of McKendrick's skull. He had become now, he said, the character 'Vamp.' In court, Menzies was asked, 'Are you telling us that you now believe you are a vampire?' He replied, 'Yes.' 'And do you believe that you will gain immortality? Again Menzies replied, 'Yes.'

Whether or not Menzies truly believed that 'Akasha' was in communication with him and that he had become a vampire by drinking human blood is unclear. It was seen by some as an attempt to influence the jury into believing that he was not wholly in his right mind when he murdered McKendrick. But what is clear is that the idea and attraction of vampirism is today a powerful motif, one that undoubtedly exercises a strong influence on certain minds. Allan Menzies was, and is,not alone in believing that he could turn himself into a vampire. In Germany, Daniel Ruda and his wife Manuela murdered Frank Hackert in 2001. Hackert was killed as a sacrifice so that the Rudas could prove that they had become vampires and were worthy of acceptance into vampire hell. What is equally chilling is that the couple claimed to have learned about vampirism, and had conceived the idea that they could become vampires, during the time that they had spent living in Scotland. It isn't clear exactly who was instructing them and it was suspected that the couple were, in fact, trying to conceal the names of those they had been in contact with during the years they had lived here. It can be guessed why.

One other factor should be considered in the Menzies and Ruda cases. Did some weird being enter our world and set out to twist each of their minds and so encourage them to carry out unspeakable acts? Menzies claimed that Akasha had an almost physical presence. Weird though that undoubtedly seems, in a sense it is no more strange than a host of bizarre entities people have claimed to have encountered, just more disturbing. If individuals meet with goblins, fairies, ghosts and aliens is that any different, in essence, from being faced with a being claiming to be a vampire? Allan Menzies was found guilty of murder and sentenced to a minimum of eighteen years in prison. But, in November 2004, he was found dead in in Shotts prison having succeeded in hanging himself. It was a mystery how he managed it. Or had Akasha, or whoever was claiming to be Akasha, returned to claim him for the vampire world, just as she had promised?

In her book, *Vampire Nation*, writer Arlene Russo highlights the fact that we should not consider 'the vampire' but rather 'vampirism', as there are different types of vampires. Some are not afraid of sunlight and the drive to turn others into the 'undead' through sucking their blood is by no means a universal trait. In the folklore of some countries, people became vampires in a variety of ways and do not have to be bitten by a vampire to be turned into one. However, there are certain characteristics which, to my mind, define the creature. True vampires can only be those who having died have risen again and who then sustain their activities through sucking the blood or devouring the flesh of a living human being. There are those today who claim to be vampires though they have never experienced death. I would suggest that this group do not classify as 'real' vampires, whatever else they may be. Nor would the true vampire, as some do today, advertise their activities as, though they may have control over their thoughts, they are driven by the irresistible compulsion to, literally, live off other people. They cannot, therefore, by their very nature, walk the streets announcing their vampirism although they may secretly associate with fellow vampires. The type of life a vampire leads has to be concealed as, otherwise, they would most certainly find their 'lifestyle' curtailed. If vampires once existed they may still do so today, but, rest assured, they won't be inviting you to a public house to discuss their way of life, or try to convince you that beneath it all they are really 'normal' people. In any case, an entity which owes its existence to some type of paranormal origin should, in my view, be treated warily, no matter what others may suggest.

But vampires on the streets of Edinburgh? Whenever we think of such a being our minds surely turn to the mountains and distant valleys of Eastern Europe, faraway places like Transylvania and the like. Strangely, however, the writer we most associate with vampirism, Bram Stoker, whose iconic novel, *Dracula* has created a lasting impression was moved to write his book after visiting Slaines Castle on Scotland's east coast, north of Aberdeen. Certainly it is a haunting place and few who visit it can come away without being affected by its brooding presence. But Stoker does not appear to have connected Scotland to the activities of the vampire. Instead, he looked to Eastern Europe and set up a link to the origin of this beast which has firmly burned itself on our consciousness.

All of which is rather strange because, in past centuries, it was Scotland rather than the east of Europe which was seen as a hotbed of vampire activity. And, indeed, there are numerous instances from across the land, which suggest belief in, and the actions of, a vampire. Edinburgh did not escape their presence and, pulling back years of accumulated misinterpretation, we can see just how strong the vampire motif was present.

Once we start to take the idea of the vampire seriously, previously unexplained incidents can be seen in a different light. William Christie Miller, who died in 1848, was the last in line of a Quaker family. His father and grandfather had been amazingly successful businessmen whose ability to turn a profit was the talk of the city. Having inherited the family fortune, William enjoyed a luxurious lifestyle, living on a large estate in Craigentinny. But for someone who had everything to live for William was seen as a rather strange character. He lived a solitary life and did not marry. His main interest was his library. He gathered a vast number of books, many dealing with the occult, and was said to spend much of his time researching a variety of bizarre subjects, though exactly what remains a mystery. And, of course, it could simply be the sort of rumour which can arise when a wealthy person keeps himself to himself and lives his life away from the public gaze. He was an odd-looking figure, very thin with spindly limbs and a high voice. He was, it was said, also completely hairless. But strange though his behaviour appeared in life, in death he left an even greater mystery. William Miller left strict instructions in his will that

The mausoleum where William Christie's grave lies. Why did he insist on being buried forty feet underground?

he had to be buried at night and most definitely not during the hours of daylight.

Miller could not hide the fact that he was having a tomb built for his body after death. Indeed, it hardly seemed remarkable that a rich man would chose to do anything else. But what people would have wondered at, had it been general knowledge, was that beneath the monument to mark the site of his grave a shaft had been dug into the ground which was over forty feet deep, many times deeper than necessary for a normal burial. Even stranger for a religious man of the period, he ordered that the tomb must be dug on open land and not in a churchyard. Secret instruction, it was claimed, had been given to his solicitor that his coffin must be made of lead, sealed completely and placed at the very bottom of the shaft. In a final touch, a stone slab several inches thick was placed over the coffin. It can surely be stated with some certainty that Miller did not want anyone to have easy access to his body .

The marble mausoleum which surmounts Miller's grave boasts some remarkable scenes of a religious type, including 'The overthrow of the pharaoh in the Red Sea' and 'The Song of Miriam and Moses'. These obviously meant something to Miller though exactly what is not clear. Both designs refer to the swamping of the pharaoh's army while crossing the Red Sea as they pursued the fleeing Moses, so there is in both a connection with Ancient Egypt, in which Miller was interested, and a more general lesson of good triumphing over evil. There may well be a deeper and hidden meaning, but it awaits discovery. The mausoleum still stands, its brooding presence dominating a row of pre-war bungalows on Craigentinny Crescent.

But did Miller rest in peace? Rumours claiming to explain the real reasons for the strange burial swept the city. It was said that Miller was overly worried about the possible action of bodysnatchers and that, as a wealthy man, he was more likely than most to be a target of these gruesome gangs. But even if that were true the precautions he took seemed, to others, extreme. A more perceptive view expressed by some, held that Miller had something to hide. Could that have been some bizarre family secret? Was Miller terrified that he might rise again from his tomb? Turn into something unspeakable? Even arise as one of the undead? It seems unlikely and sceptics have drawn attention to the fact that Miller asked that his coffin be sealed thoroughly which suggests, if anything, that he was more afraid of something getting in rather than getting out. Unless, of course, he was anxious to ensure that he himself did not emerge from the casket. And, in any case, vampires have, as do all supernatural entities, the ability to pass through solid matter; a characteristic remarked on since time immemorial.

However, it might be wrong to dismiss it all as a flight of fancy. An incident from the 1940s, suggests that whatever lay at the root of Miller's behaviour something strange was going on at his grave. Bill McDonald, a former policeman, relates how one night a colleague was patrolling along the street where Miller's memorial stands when he noticed that the door on the memorial was open. He had patrolled the area regularly so realised at once that it should be shut and that clearly something was 'not right'. Switching on his torch he edged inside then shone the beam down the deep shaft. At the very bottom he glimpsed a figure moving around. The shock was too much and, not waiting to learn more, he rapidly exited the chamber slamming the door shut behind him. Had something got out, or was something trying to get into, or re-enter, Miller's grave? Or was it all simply a trick of the light?

Vampires are notoriously elusive. Encounters are infrequent and to get a broader view of the activities of these entities, and what they might be up to in the city, it's useful to gather information from incidents from a number of sites not too far away. In Melrose some time ago a priest had become notorious for his behaviour, especially over a series of sexual liaisons. When he died his phantom was seen wandering about the town although it appeared more substantial and solid than a simple apparition. And so it turned out as one night when the priest went into the bedroom of a local woman and attacked her, with quite obvious sexual intent. She recognised him and as she described it he was not like any 'spirit' she could have imagined and had become almost like a living being again. She survived the assault only because her screams attracted attention. But there was general concern that he was likely to attack again so it was agreed to keep watch over the priest's grave. They didn't have to wait long as, on the following night, the priest rose from the ground as if alive again. He immediately attacked those at his graveside and they defended themselves eventually sinking an axe into the priest's chest. He sank back into his grave, but as it was still dark it was felt that it would be safer to wait till daylight before taking further action. When they opened the priest's coffin the next day his body looked quite fresh, not that of a dead man. They could plainly see the blood still flowing from the axe wound. They took him out and burned his body to ashes; the most sensible way to deal with such a creature.

Some miles further east, a community experienced an equally bizarre attack. During the time that Berwick on Tweed was ruled by Scottish kings it was terrorised by a strange creature; a man who had died, but who had come back to life again. According to a report of the time:

> After he was buried he used to, at night, emerge from his grave and rush up and down the streets of the town. Anyone who met him was terrified and nobody wanted to step outside their house till daybreak when the creature returned to his coffin.

Eventually it was agreed that the situation could not be allowed to continue. A group of people came together and went to the grave. They dug up the body, cut it into bits then burned the whole lot in a furnace. This 'living corpse' had the character-istics of a vampire though there was no evidence that it was feeding on the blood of the living — the traditional hallmark of the undead.

But other incidents make it clear that a supply of blood was believed to be an essential ingredient in resurrecting the dead. In the Dumfriesshire town of Annan a dead man, even though interred with Christian rites, rose from the grave to torment the town. An eyewitness of the time reported that: 'going out from his tomb in the night time he used to wander through the streets and around the houses from the fall of darkness to the rising of the sun.' Two brothers decided to deal with the creature and went to the spot where he was buried. They expected to have to dig deep to reach his body, but were surprised to find that he was lying not far from the surface. The corpse was swollen and the face red as if it had been gorging on blood. And, indeed, when they started hacking at the body, fresh blood ran from the wounds, evidence that the vampire had been feeding on the living, though it was unclear exactly who his victims had been. The body was dismembered and the pieces thrown on a bonfire. The only way to ensure that a vampire would cause no more trouble was to destroy completely its physical body.

An encounter close to the Scottish border with England also suggests that we are dealing with a flesh-and-blood entity and brings us closer to the present era. In the village of Croglin, in the latter part of the nineteenth century, a woman was attacked one night by a strange-looking creature with a brown face and flaming eyes. The creature bit her on the throat, but ran off when she screamed. Some months later it appeared again at her window and her brother shot it in the leg. They watched it disappear over the churchyard wall into a family vault. When the vault was opened they found a brown, mummified figure in a coffin, with a recent gunshot wound to the leg.

In the nineteenth century, in Forfar, following the death of her boyfriend, his fiancée insisted on being buried beside him in a double coffin. A few days after the burial she ordered that the grave be opened and lowered herself inside, determined that she would stay with her beloved's corpse even though she was still alive and healthy.

She had dressed herself in white like a bride going to a wedding, but must have known that death awaited her. Not long after people walking through woods close to the graveyard claimed to see a white-gowned female hovering among the trees waving and beckoning to them. It was believed that the young woman had guessed that her boyfriend was a vampire and decided that she had to be reunited with him, even if this meant allowing him her own blood and becoming herself a vampire in the process. Now, of course, they both needed fresh victims to sustain themselves.

A bizarre tale from Strathy, though it involves the wife of a minister, is suggestive of the resurrection of the 'living corpse'. The woman, dead and laid out in the living room, was viewed by many people. She appeared quite lifeless, though in death she still managed to look young and attractive. The woman was buried, but local thieves decided to raid the grave and steal the rings she had been interred with. On the same night as the funeral they opened the lair and took off the coffin lid. But as they worked, the corpse started to move. The men took off. In the account it seems that the woman returned to her husband covered in blood. She remained alive for many years and even had children. So what had been the fate of the two thieves who, apparently, disappeared without trace? The implication is that, in reality, she had feasted on their blood in order to come back to life. Items of value had been buried with her and talked about openly, probably in order to encourage thieves to visit the graveside. If known wrongdoers vanished, there would be few to worry about their fate. But there is, of course, a puzzle.

How did the woman sustain herself thereafter? Was there more secret bloodletting? Or does the evidence imply that she needed only one quantity of fresh blood to bring her back to life? This is not the behaviour of the traditional vampire as we know it, but there may be, for all we know of the nature of this creature, a variety of types, some of which may need only the occasional intake of blood to maintain their bizarre existence.

These reports from across Scotland suggest a widespread tradition of vampire encounters. But Scotland also had a theme more in keeping with the modern view of the vampire phenomenon, as depicted in several films. These were women who dressed in long, flowing, green dresses. Attractive and seductive, they would lure young men to them and sink their sharp teeth into their flesh, sucking the blood of their victims. They were, in reality, old hags who maintained their youthful looks by consuming the blood of the young people they seduced and attacked. They did not usually kill their victims, but left severe wounds on their necks and shoulders, wounds that would not heal, though their victims do not appear to have turned into vampires themselves. These women, known as Boabhan Sith, could be kept away by the presence of a horse.

However, though these incidents are strong evidence of a vampire tradition and presence they are, it has to be said, incidents from more rural locations; spots where a vampire could easily slip into the night or where sheer isolation may over stimulate the imagination. But what about the 'undead' stalking the streets of Scotland's ancient capital? The mind does find it hard to adjust to the idea, but several incidents lead to the inevitable conclusion that the tradition of vampirism lurks not too far beneath the surface. And the incident of the Edinburgh butcher who allegedly saw an apparition of his wife can surely be seen in a different light when the characteristics of the vampire are taken into consideration. The tradition goes that the man's wife died mysteriously while in her early thirties, leaving her husband with a young family to take care of. He was still a young man himself and, naturally, began to look around for female companionship which he found with a neighbour or two. One evening, while he was sitting in his flat speaking to a female friend, he glanced up at the window and saw an apparition of his wife standing at the window watching him. But it was an apparition of the strangest kind as it appeared solid with a waxy-hued face and trailing burial clothes, as if it had just emerged from the grave. The butcher was terrified by the encounter and stayed away from the house for several days. When he returned he was again confronted by a sighting of his dead wife at the window staring at him. The next sequence of events is unclear. The butcher fell into some kind of unexplained illness during which the life force seemed to drain slowly from him and he grew gradually more pale. It has been claimed that strange marks appeared on his body, but there is no clear description of where they were located or what they looked like. Bite marks of a resurrected vampire? One who wanted her husband to join her as one of the undead? It can only be speculation, but there is certainly more to this tale than is obvious at first glance. To put it down as simply another haunting ignores the more sinister aspects to the event.

The same applies to the bizarre series of events surrounding the death of Sir James Stanfield. On 20 November 1686, Stanfield's body was seen floating on the River Tyne in East Lothian by John Topping, who claimed to be just passing through the district. However, Topping later reported that Stanfield's son Philip was standing on the river bank simply watching the body drift by and making no effort to pull him from the water. He also denied to Topping that he had recognised the corpse. In fact, Philip went to the home of his father's friend, a minister, John Bell, and asked him if he knew where his father was. This was clearly strange behaviour as he had seen the body in the river and Topping knew that he had been there. It seems obvious that for some reason Philip wanted to be absolutely sure that Stanfield was dead, regardless of whether or not he was himself implicated in his father's death. It begs the question: Why? Was there something about his father which worried him so much that he was careless about his own life? Events would shortly reveal more strange aspects to the affair. Soon after Philip's meeting with John Bell, Stanfield's body was discovered and fished from the river. It seems that John Topping had failed to report his sighting of the body and, in another odd twist, it appears he was never properly questioned on the matter. It may, in fact, have made little difference to the fate of James Stanfield whether or not he was pulled from the river. Stanfield had, in fact, been murdered, though Philip seemed anxious to deny it and swore that his father had simply drowned in a tragic accident.

With his father's body back in the house, Philip began to act in a rash and bizarre way. He ransacked his father's private rooms as if looking for something, then burned books and documents. At some point during the night he went to an outhouse where his father's body was lying, took it out and buried it in a local churchyard. If Philip had set out to attract attention he could not have gone about it in a more obvious way. It seems clear that he was out to hide something. But what could it have been?

In Edinburgh, where the family was well known and connected, concern grew that Sir James had died an unnatural death. The Lord Advocate ordered Stanfield's body to be exhumed and examined. On Monday, 30 November, Sir James's body was removed from the ground and taken into the church. A post-mortem was carried out, but it's obvious that the whole event had been stage-managed to carry out a bizarre test. Philip was ordered to touch his father's body. As he placed his hand as instructed blood gushed from the left side of Stanfield's neck. Philip staggered back in shock and those gathered round were just as stunned by what they had witnessed. They had every reason to be amazed as it is physically impossible for blood to flow from a dead person. Even in those far-off days that fact was well known. And James Stanfield had, by now, been dead for several days. All of which suggests that either everyone had made a terrible mistake and Stanfield was still somehow alive, which goes against all the recorded facts, or, just as weird, some strange transformation had taken place in Stanfield which had reactivated his corpse. Had he been turned into a vampire? In which case, the blood that poured from him would have been the blood he had sucked from the victims he had gorged on. But in that case there would be, it would be thought, evidence of attacks on individuals in the area and there is nothing in the records I have been able to discover that would link obviously to vampire attacks. However, maybe Stanfield was in the process of transformation or any assaults had been carried out further away. Or maybe the rumours at the time that Stanfield had been some kind of blood-sucking beast were way off the mark.

But there are other aspects of the case that require explanation. At his trial in February 1688, at the High Court in the city, Philip was accused of strangling his father. However, as the post-mortem had shown there was a wound of some kind on Stanfield's neck out of which blood had flowed. So how had that got there? Had Stanfield been the victim of a separate attack of some kind? The issue was ignored. People were puzzled, but no one enquired too deeply. But the way that Philip was dealt with raised further question marks over this whole strange affair. Found guilty after a three-day trial he was sentenced to death. After his death, however, the authorities refused to allow his body to be buried. Oddly, it was secretly cut down and found floating in the water in a nearby pond, in an echo of the circumstances in which his father's body had been discovered. Was this someone's idea of justice or some sort of strange ceremony intended to 'cleanse' the body or nullify some evil, in the same way that witches, it is said, were unable to survive immersion in running water? It's odd too that his tongue and right hand were cut off. What was this meant to signify? Philip's body then disappeared and was never found. Had Philip, too, become one of the undead and found a secret hiding place? Or had someone set out to make sure that Philip Stanfield could never rise again and so obliterated his remains for all time? Whether or not the Stanfield clan were a family of vampires, it's interesting that the tradition of the blood-sucking 'undead' was well established at the time.

In fact, it might be thought that Bram Stoker, who was a regular visitor to Scotland, had no need to travel as far as Slaines Castle for inspiration. There was plenty happening in and around Edinburgh to raise his curiosity. And who knows . . . maybe it did. There's a report about events in a house in Inverleith, owned by William Brien, which certainly are suggestive of a vampire presence. Brien lived alone in a large house of ten rooms and was never seen to go out during the day. No one seemed to visit him apart from a cleaner who called from time to time. He was a mystery man and the enigma deepened on his death. All the neighbours saw was a coffin being removed from the house by undertakers they did not recognise, then taken to a destination that was not revealed. Equally as puzzling were the actions of William's cleaner. She had keys to the house and was seen to lock all the windows and double bolt both the front and back doors. If no one could get in, no one could have got out easily either. The cleaner then vanished and never reappeared and the house, grand as it was, began to deteriorate gradually over the next few years, with obvious signs of neglect as paint withered from the door.

But was the house empty? Neighbours on either side began to wonder as noises were heard through the walls. Was it significant these were normally heard during the hours of darkness and especially after midnight? And voices too, both men and women's, could be heard even though people were certain that no one went into Brien's house, no lights could be seen and, during the day, the whole house seemed quite dead. However, no one bothered to investigate and the house was left in peace.

At some point, however, and after many years, the house was sold, but a lot of time had passed since Brien had died and World War I was underway. The house was done up as a boarding house and rooms were let to unsuspecting visitors. The house soon revealed that whatever had lurked there had not gone away. Had the sale been a ploy to attract innocent victims? Was someone or something hiding in one of the attic rooms? One of the staff reported hearing voices coming from one of these chambers. When she went to look, however, there was no one there. A cleaner had the same experience, but also felt an invisible presence standing next to her, so intense and evil that she believed it was trying to take control of her mind. She felt, she said 'almost hypnotised.' Vampires, it should be noted, have the power of invisibility and try to 'take over' a person before attacking them. In the light of these events it was decided that it would not be advisable to let the room so it was kept empty.

However, it is sometimes hard for a hotel owner to turn business away and a young couple desperate for accommodation were given the room, as it was the only one unoccupied. When they went up to it they heard voices. They guessed a mistake had been made and called for help. Mary Brewster was the staff member who came in response. Knowing the room must be empty she walked straight in and saw something that utterly shocked her. When the owner rushed up on hearing her shrieks he found her clutching the end of the bed and gazing up at the attic window as if something had just disappeared through it. Mary was in a badly shaken state and refused to discuss what she had seen. She left and never came back.

Then Andrew Muir arrived. He was a student who had an interest in the supernatural and was desperate to see what was causing the incidents in the room. With the owner's agreement he sat there one night on his own. He had a bell with him which he would ring if he saw the presence of an entity. The owner heard the bell ring and rushed to the room hoping to see the 'ghost'. Instead he found the body of Andrew Muir slumped in a chair with, according to some reports, blood running from his shoulder and neck. The incident was certainly hushed up. No one, as far as I have been able to discover, was charged with Andrew's murder. Andrew Muir was a medical student at Edinburgh University. If he had graduated it would be a straightforward matter to confirm his details, but as he died while still a student it's all a little harder to confirm. It has to be acknowledged that, as often is the case, details may have added over the years, but, nonetheless, it's hard to deny that the events at Inverleith make up a very strange set of incidents which have 'vampire' written all over them.

But a question that seems reasonable to ask is, if there are vampires, where are they all coming from? And where do they all hide? To answer that let us consider another question. Were the notorious killers, Burke and Hare, blamed unfairly? There's no doubt that the pair were guilty of several murders apparently for the purpose of supplying bodies for medical dissection, and that they also robbed a few graves. But the number of bodies that were going missing from graveyards suggests an event that went beyond the activities of two criminals too inept to escape detection. According to tradition, bodies were disappearing at an extraordinary rate because medical schools were in need of corpses for dissection. But, it should be asked, how much use was a body which had been decaying for several days and been buried in the ground? And can it really be said that all the bodies that vanished were required by medical science? The number of medical students in Edinburgh, during the 1820s, at the time of Burke and Hare, was tiny. As was the number of teaching doctors. The disappearance of the dead from city graveyards far exceeded the needs of the medical fraternity at this time. And the amazing skills alleged to be possessed by grave robbers is an added puzzling aspect. In spite of all the precautions taken, including watch towers and night patrols, bodies kept disappearing, According to reports from the time the grave robbers were so skilled that they could dig up a body several feet under, remove the corpse and fill in the grave so rapidly that the actions passed unnoticed until the plot was examined carefully, maybe days later. The ability of the grave robber to carry out his gruesome task and get clean away undetected was a wonder of the time.

But could there be another explanation? In the 1970s, Tom Alder was passing Gorgie cemetery at the Slateford Road entrance. He glimpsed a movement just at the edge of the area lit by the street lamps, but lying in shadow. He'd passed this way at night many times and had seen people walking around the cemetery before and assumed it was teenagers larking about as a dare. But this was much later than normal and somehow it just seemed different. The person he could make out appeared oddly misshapen and, Tom explained:

Frankly it looked as if the figure was wearing some kind of cloak. A car went by and it seemed to startle 'him.' I assumed it was a 'he', but he didn't seem to notice me. It was about 1 a.m. so there wasn't anyone around and at that point I was more curious than anything. But then something totally weird happened. I know it sounds hard to believe, I can hardly believe it myself, but 'something' seemed to rise out of the ground beside the shadowy figure. My body felt like it had turned to ice in an instant. A voice in my head kept saying, 'It's just a trick. It's just a trick,' but I was petrified. There was just something so weird about it. I must have said something in the middle of all this, or done something, and the shadowy figure turned and looked straight at me stepping forward a bit more into the light. It had a human shape but spindly arms and legs. I was utterly panicking and wanted to get away, but I couldn't get anything to move. Next, I saw that the figure that had risen from the ground was facing me. It looked like a woman's shape as it had a kind of flowing garment on. All this probably happened in seconds, but it felt like a lifetime. I might have stood there forever if the woman hadn't suddenly lifted a couple of feet off the ground and seemed to hover in the air with her arms pointing towards me like a scene from a horror film. I admit I screamed. I've never been so terrified in my whole life not even while in the army. But that seemed to break the spell and I turned and ran, not along Slateford Road which was my usual route, but round the church and up Harrison Road. Any second I expected to see those creatures, but nothing else happened. My wife thought I must have drunk too much, and I had had a drink, but only a couple of pints, nothing more than usual. After that I gave Slateford Road a wide birth and it was only after several months that I plucked up courage to walk past the cemetery gates at night. Did I imagine it all? I know it may sound strange but I really hope that I did. Thinking about it sends shivers through me.

Tom's experience certainly stretches belief. I can add a personal note here. For a few years while in my early twenties, my wife, Evelyn, and I lived in a flat overlooking Gorgie cemetery, so I was particularly intrigued by Tom's account. I did occasionally see individuals walking through the graveyard at night, but never saw anything remotely strange, and the people I did see I took to be youngsters testing their nerves as many of us have no doubt done. There's no obvious short cut through the cemetery to Gorgie Road so anyone there would only go in after dark for some other reason which, of course, could be perfectly innocent. While Tom's experience is the only one of its type I'm aware of from Edinburgh I have heard of similar incidents from across Scotland, though it has to be said they are few and far between. One has, therefore, to look at the possibility that some kind of strange trick was being played out. But why? And how could anyone be sure that someone would pass at the appropriate time? Then there's the fact Tom saw the woman apparently rise from the ground. A trick of the light? Or had Tom's imagination simply got the better of him? The truth is that, once a person is dead and buried, it rarely happens that a grave is examined to make sure that the corpse is still lying in its resting place.

I've often wondered if there's any connection with the type of incident experienced by Tom and an event which took place some years later. In October 1992, in a house overlooking Niddry Burn, Moira woke up in the early hours of the morning and caught sight of an intense white light clearly visible through the window. She got out of bed to take a closer look and her attention was drawn to a tree at the foot of the garden. Crouching on a thick branch was a creature which she took at first to be a giant bird, one as big as a man. Moira was frightened and fascinated all at the same time. She wanted to step back from the window, but felt a powerful impulse as if she was unable to look away. But as she took a longer look she became aware that apart from its huge size there were other strange aspects to it. It seemed to have a mixture of human and bird type features; ordinary arms and legs, but attached to its back were two large wings. It was a disturbing experience although the entity did not seem to be aware of her presence and made no attempt to confront her. Oddly, Moira's husband slept through her sighting and couldn't be woken up. Moira, too, felt 'a bit strange', almost if she had 'walked into another world'. Admittedly, it's difficult to be sure exactly what was seen and there are various possibilities, but some traditional descriptions of vampires include beings with wings. And vampires are often portrayed as possessing bat-like character-istics even, on some occasions, turning into these beasts to attack or escape.

As the history of vampires shows, these creatures can manage remarkable transformations. They need not appear as solid flesh and blood creatures. Nor need they necessarily launch a physical attack on a human being. In fact, the psychic vampire, one which sucks the life force from a man or woman, might be a far more common entity. There are many accounts of the incubus and succubus, the strange creatures which appear during the night in the form of a man or beautiful woman, and attempt to have sexual intercourse with the occupant of the bed. But as these entities do not appear to posses real bodies is their intention, in fact, to suck out the spirit force and thereby sustain their own bizarre existence? Some claim that this is, indeed, the case and incidents from more recent times suggest that they may be right. Sandra Donald was in her forties when she experienced a messy divorce. She said:

After we split I bought a small flat in Leith. This was around August 1981. I was pleased to have a place of my own and felt

I had a start in rebuilding my life again. I really liked my new home and it was very handy for getting to town where I worked. I was in a bit of turmoil because of everything I'd been through, but there's no way that explained what happened. One day the atmosphere in the flat just seemed to change. I'd felt fine there, but after I came home from work one evening, I think it was October, the atmosphere seemed all heavy and depressed. I couldn't put my finger on it and thought it was just my imagination. But that night in bed I had a strange dream that something human-like, but not fully like a man, put his mouth over mine, but wasn't kissing me, more sucking the air from my mouth. I woke up in fright and thought I saw something, I'm not sure what, disappear out the window. I was terrified and stayed awake for ages. I thought 'you've been working too hard. It's just a daft dream.' The following night nothing happened, but the night after I had that horrible dream again. I woke up and I swear I saw what looked like that man thing again disappearing out the window, but I got a better sight of it. It looked like a man's shape, but I could see through his body. I really felt alone and vulnerable and went into the sitting room where I dozed in the chair till morning. The next night I forced myself to go to bed, left the bedside lamp on and slept right through. And I never had that dream again, though the atmosphere in the flat was still oppressive. Now I realised I was getting listless. I thought at first it was because I'd lost sleep, but I was getting a good sleep and still feeling washed out. People began telling me I looked tired and pale. And it was true. My energy seemed to be going down to nothing. I became convinced that it must be the flat. I hated to admit it because I'd been so proud of it and loved the place. I moved in with my mum though I didn't tell her why, just saying I needed some company. Two weeks later I went back to the flat and the whole feeling of the place was miles better. It made me feel better too. I was a bit nervous when I started sleeping there again, but nothing happened. The place seemed like it was back to normal. I have no idea what happened to me, but it was a horrible experience. I felt that I'd been used by something. God knows what and I'd rather not find out, to be honest.

Sandra may not have suffered long-term physical harm. She was not subjected to an assault by a blood-sucking beast, but her experience suggests that the vampire, which sets out to live on the life force of men and women, may be the one we truly have to fear. It can catch us unawares while we sleep and quietly eat away at our energy levels, and do it so gently that we remain blissfully unaware of its presence.

5

Contacting 'Other Worlds'

In the Royal Mile there once stood a statue to one of the city's weirdest exports. Daniel Home may no longer be a household name, but in the nineteenth century he was internationally famous. A friend to royalty and the rich in Britain, the United States, and Russia, he was born in Currie in March 1833, and raised in Portobello by his aunt. His family had emigrated to the USA while he was still a baby leaving Daniel behind. Daniel's mother was herself a psychic and he believed that it was through her — she came from Highland stock — that he inherited his amazing psychic powers. From his father he claimed a different and exalted pedigree. Daniel was told by his parents that he was descended from the Home family of the Borders, the ancestors of Sir Alec Douglas-Home who became the British Prime Minister in 1963. The account he was told was that his father was the illegitimate son of a member of the Home family and a servant, following an illicit affair. The Home family, naturally, never admitted to it and it may be untrue, but there's no doubt that Daniel Home believed it and boasted openly of his distinguished ancestry.

Home's first psychic experience occurred in Portobello when he was no more than four years old. A cousin who lived several miles away appeared to him in a vision. The phantom spoke to Daniel and told him that he had passed into another place, but when Daniel told of what he had seen no one believed him. It turned out though that the spectre had told the truth when he reported his own death, and young Daniel was looked at in a different light thereafter. There were other strange incidents. His aunt claimed that when he was a baby voices could be heard in his room when there was no one there, and invisible hands would gently rock his cradle.

After a period in the United States, Home returned to Britain in 1855. His reputation as a psychic medium went before him and he was soon holding seances, which were attended by well-known figures of the day, including Sir David Brewster, Scotland's foremost scientist and a graduate of Edinburgh University. Brewster was amazed by Home's psychic ability and encouraged others to investigate Daniel and see for themselves. Home soon found himself in even more exalted company, contacting the spirits of the dead for the Emperor Napoleon III of France, Queen Sophia of Holland and the Tsar of Russia, among other aristocrats of Europe. The man of humble origins from Edinburgh had most certainly arrived.

So what was it about Daniel Home that marked him out from other psychics? Or were these rarified circles the dupes of a cunning individual who pretended to paranormal powers he did not really possess? The controversy, which began in Home's lifetime, has rumbled on to the present. Hundreds of witnesses attended Home's seances and claimed to have seen events which defied reality. In broad daylight people said they saw Home float from the ground and drift up to the ceiling. He did this many times, but sceptics still refused to believe it. Home claimed that the spirits of the dead were present at his seances and it was these beings that, taking hold of his arms, raised him many feet off the floor.

In 1869, he carried out the most bizarre feat of his whole career. In the presence of several distinguished witnesses, including members of the House of Lords, Home floated off the ground and then drifted horizontally through a gap between the window and the sill, hovering thirty feet above the pavement outside. The space his body squeezed through was no more than eighteen inches wide and some even suggested that he had gone straight through the glass window. Home, however, had previously demonstrated the ability to lengthen his body and become much thinner in the process, a feat which on its own defies common sense, but was witnessed by dozens of individuals. Lord Adare who was present and published an account of the event, could offer no explanation of how Home had managed it, but noted that, after drifting in mid-air outside the building for a few minutes, Home simply floated back in through another window.

Was it some kind of mass hallucination? It might seem to be the answer except that scientists who tested Home came to believe in his extraordinary powers. Sir William Crookes, the discoverer of the element thallium, conducted what he believed to be tamper-proof experiments with Home in his laboratory. Afterwards, he had no doubt that he had demonstrated that Home possessed unexplained abilities including that of making musical instruments play without touching them and changing the weight of objects simply by looking at them. He also wrote of how Home materialised a glowing hand which put a piece of shining crystal into Crooke's palm, and confirmed that he had watched Home float from the ground at will. When Crookes published his findings several prominent scientists ridiculed him and he was forced to end his experiments. He never doubted what he had seen, however, and would quietly confirm it in private conversation.

Meanwhile, Home's life moved on. He abandoned his work with scientists convinced that no matter what mystical incidents they witnessed they would always doubt, or even deny, what they had seen. But in less demanding circles people could not get enough of him. He was invited to the greatest houses in the land because of his ability to relay messages from the spirit world and materialise phantoms, that would be instantly recognised by those present as their departed relatives. Either people were easily fooled, or deluding themselves, or something truly strange was going on. Many people, including MPs, writers and businessmen, came to his seances again and again. Whatever he was doing to produce such bizarre phenomena it must have been convincing to attract such an important clientele.

When Home died in 1886 his wife, knowing of his attachment to Edinburgh, gave the City Council the then vast sum of £4,000 to set up a memorial to her husband. The statue was erected outside Canongate Parish Church where it stood till the early 1950s, by which time it had fallen into disrepair. It then disappeared till some years later it was tracked down by an *Evening News* reporter who found it lying in a builder's scrap yard. It was never re-erected, though part of it found a home at the Edinburgh College of Parapsychology. Maybe the time has arrived to honour afresh the memory of Daniel Home, one of the city's most famous sons, and to put up a new monument in his name.

Psychics tell us that interacting with the spirit world can be a dangerous business for the uninitiated. You need to make sure that you are protected from the physical and mental effect of crossing the paths of entities from other dimensions. Was this a warning Hugh Miller chose to ignore? Miller was a self-taught genius of the nineteenth century, who contributed to many fields including science, religion and the paranormal. He was admired by many and in contact with leading people of the time, including Andrew Carnegie and the founder of environmentalism, John Muir, among others. *The Encyclopaedia of*

The grave of Hugh Miller scientist and writer with a world-wide reputation. So why did he feel so terrorised by demons from other worlds that he committed suicide?

Scotland describes him as no less than 'an icon in many disciplines'.

Hugh Miller was not born in Edinburgh, originating further north on the edge of the Cromarty Firth. But he eventually settled in the capital where he edited a newspaper *The Witness*. By this time he had earned a reputation as a scientific writer and as a man who was attempting to reconcile the theory of evolution with events in the Bible. Miller was, by all accounts, happily married to his wife Lydia, who had borne him four children. The family lived in a house in Portobello known as 'Shrub Mount', which he had purchased in April 1854. It stood on the shore side of the High Street and was described at the time as 'an eighteenth-century cottage with its own grounds.' With an established reputation, Miller seemed to have everything to live for and was in demand as a speaker and writer.

So why did events take such a bizarre turn? On 23 December 1856, Miler, as he often did, helped his daughter Harriet with her school homework. He then read aloud to the children, poems by William Cowper, one of the best loved poets of the time. After going upstairs to his study where he sat for a while he then went into his bedroom, located next door, to rest. It was all a part of his normal everyday routine. At some time during the night, however, Hugh Miller went back to his study, pulled up the fisherman's jersey he was wearing, placed a gun to his chest and blasted a bullet through his body.

Why he did this aroused a controversy which inflames passions to this day. Although it might have been thought that the sound of gunfire would have immediately alerted the household, Miller's corpse was not discovered until the following morning. Foul play was at no point suspected. His wife Lydia claimed that, on discovering the body, her first thought was that a tragic accident had taken place. Hugh, she guessed, had been playing with the gun and it had gone off by accident. Incredibly she missed the note Hugh had left for her, which was lying on his desk; a note which told a different tale. It was the Reverend Thomas Guthrie, a family friend who, having gone to the house on hearing the news, drew Lydia's attention to the message, which certainly suggested that something had tipped Miller over the edge. The note read:

Dearest Lydia,
My brain burns. I *must* have *walked;* and a fearful dream rises upon me. I cannot bear the horrible thought. God and father of the Lord Jesus Christ have mercy on me. Dearest Lydia, dear

children farewell. My brain burns as the recollection grows. My dear, dear wife, farewell.
Hugh Miller.

An observer might well wonder just exactly what Hugh Miller was talking about. It certainly wasn't obvious to his wife and friends. A post-mortem was carried out which added little to what is known of the event. It stated that Miller's brain had a diseased appearance and that he had killed himself while temporarily insane. The disease referred to was not specified so whether it had any relevance to the events is unclear.

So was Miller suffering from temporary insanity? Certainly the scientific world where his name is still revered would like to think so. They would hate to admit that their hero succumbed to a far more weird death, that he was a man taunted and frightened by the spirits and entities of those other worlds which he had, throughout his life, believed in. And it seems, communicated with. There's no doubt that in the last few months of his life, Miller was convinced that the demons of the spirit domains were closing in on him. He seemed unable to escape them.

One of Miller's most widely read books then and now was his *Scenes and Legends of Northern Scotland,* published in 1835. Miller had gathered together a large collection of 'folk tales', many of which had a supernatural basis. It was an odd thing for a scientist to do. But, of course, at the time Miller had not earned a reputation for his work in geology, for which he was so later admired by the scientific community. One result of this has been the refusal of scientists to accept that Miller really believed that the incidents he recounted had actually happened, in much the same way that the genius Isaac Newton's fascination with astrology and alchemy is played down, as it is seen as demeaning to anyone who claims to possess a scientific outlook, and certainly not something to be linked to a world-famous scientist.

The problem is that Miller seemed to really believe in the paranormal incidents he wrote of. He even described a strange event that he had been personally involved in. It happened when his father, a fisherman, was out at sea. He recalled:

> There were no forebodings in our house as a [letter from my father] had just been received. My mother was sitting on the evening after, beside the household fire, plying the cheerful needle, when the house door, which had been left unfastened, fell open, and I was despatched from her side to shut it. What followed must be regarded as simply the recollection, though a vivid one, of a boy who had completed his fifth year only a month before. Day had not wholly disappeared, but it was fast posting on to night when I saw at the open door less a yard off my breast, as plainly as ever I saw anything, a dissevered hand and arm stretched towards me. Hand and arm were those of a female. They bore a livid and sodden appearance and directly fronting me where the body ought to have been there was only blank, transparent space, through which I could see the dim forms of objects beyond.

Hugh screamed in fright and ran to his mother. It was an incident which affected him in later years, as the event coincided with the death of his father, lost at sea. It was as if a phantom from the world beyond was letting him know of his parent's passing from this life to the next.

It's unclear exactly what, if any, visions Miller experienced in later life, but it seems irrefutable that he did so. He talked of 'fairies' visiting his garden and he did not mean the later, winged Victorian invention, but the more human-like entities famously described by the Reverend Robert Kirk in his epic work, *The Secret Commonwealth of Elves, Fauns and Fairies* published in 1691; beings who though they appear almost identical to humans, inhabit a parallel universe, but can enter ours at will. Hugh's wife, Lydia, who it seems reasonable to assume knew him as well as anyone, wrote in her biography of her husband that his mother had filled his mind with tales of demons and other beings, which had the effect of depressing his mind. There seems no doubt then that Hugh Miller took such tales seriously as, during 1856, this 'other world' was impinging more and more on his daily life. He did, according to friends, get increasingly nervous about what they assumed were people invading his garden, and he seemed overly fearful that they would get into his house. They guessed he was worried about losing his extensive fossil collection, but would he have been so concerned about this that he bought himself a gun and ammunition? Was the weapon really intended to ward off the denizens of other worlds? Or had he come to the conclusion that only through his own death could he end the visions of those strange, disturbing entities that seemed determined to impose themselves on his thoughts?

The fate of Hugh Miller and the fame of Daniel Home show that belief in the supernatural was widespread in nineteenth-century Edinburgh. Individuals, who could not in any way be described as 'fanciful', expressed their belief that mankind was not the sole inhabitant of the planet. A leading figure in the revival of 'magic' as a dynamic force was Lewis Spence. A graduate of Edinburgh University and an editor on the *Scotsman* newspaper he set out —using his home at 66, Arden Street as a base — to argue for the importance of magic ritual in human history. As a member of the 'Golden Dawn' (a society which put magic ritual into practice) and a supporter of the monthly journal the *Occult Review*, Spence was in a key position, through his journalistic contacts, to encourage a wider interest in the whole area of the paranormal. His best known publication *The Encyclopedia of Occultism,* published in 1929 and still in print, draws out the part played by 'magic' in every aspect of daily life and in societies across the world. An active Druid, Spence was responsible for the introduction of magic rites into Druidic ritual and was Chief of the Druid Order of Britain. He was a firm believer in the lost continent of Atlantis and wrote a book arguing for its existence. He influenced the views of mystics across the world. It was a sign of the times that Spence, although he held outlandish views, was still able to mix in academic circles and be accepted by academic institutions as an expert; a situation unlikely to re-occur in the twenty-first century where the battle lines between science and magic are more tightly drawn.

Spence seemed reluctant to admit to any encounters with entities from other worlds, unlike the well-known Edinburgh artist John Duncan, whose life spans the period from the last quarter of the nineteenth century to the middle of the twentieth. His writings reveal a man obsessed with the interaction between this world and the spirit domains. His mission, as he saw it, was to produce works of art that would demonstrate this contact with the mystical realms. He wished passionately to paint the figure of Columba, the early Christian missionary, standing on the mound on the island of Iona which the Saint, as he was to become, visited regularly, and where he would be approached by, and communicate with, angels and other entities from the beyond. Duncan had experienced similar encounters himself on the island and longed to present these images to the public.

Although fairies are seen regularly even today few are willing to admit to seeing such unlikely beings. Duncan, however, revelled in his sightings of the nature spirits. He was a key figure in the magazine the *Evergreen*, which set out to revive interest in the ancient Celts and their traditions. His compatriot Lewis Spence drew out the significance of the title *Evergreen,* explaining that, 'in Druidic times people decorated their houses with evergreen plants so that the nature spirits could retire there during the winter.' To Duncan the fairies were no myth, but real beings. He had seen them and set out to show he had done so by including them in his paintings, examples of which can be seen in the National Gallery of Scotland. Duncan's fascination with the 'other world' of fauns and fairies was not shared by the public, although his pictures were widely admired, but he influenced a generation of mystics, including Robert Crombie, whose encounters with a legion of nature spirits are covered elsewhere in this book.

John Duncan did not claim to have conversed with the phantoms he saw. Helen Duncan, on the other hand, — no relation of John — was most definitely out to contact entities from 'other worlds'. Scotland's most famous female mystic, Helen Duncan was not a native of the city, but a notorious episode of her career as a spiritualist medium did take place in the capital. And at the time it caused a worldwide sensation.

Duncan is best known for being, in 1944, charged under the witchcraft act of 1736; the last person to be dealt with in this way. But although the use of this ancient law against an individual and the guilty verdict were both harsh and unfair, they were in their way a backhanded compliment to Duncan's psychic ability. Helen had revealed at a seance in Portsmouth, through the spirit of a deceased sailor, that a ship of the Royal Navy, *HMS Barham,* had been sunk by enemy action. The news that Helen had somehow found this out caused consternation in official circles as it was supposed to be a state secret. If she had learnt about this disaster what else might she discover? During the Cold War the CIA in the United States took part in a secret project to use the paranormal powers of psychics to spy on Soviet Russia. But in the 1940s, the secret services in World War II Britain simply saw Helen Duncan as a potential threat to national security. As a result she was arrested and put on trial. It was no doubt a shattering moment for Helen emotionally, but it raised her profile to star levels. Overnight, she became the most famous medium in Britain.

But that would never have been predicted back in the 1930s, when Helen's reputation as a medium was under threat. Up till then she had been building up a profile as a psychic of real ability. At her seances she exuded the substance known as 'ectoplasm', which would form slowly into spirit beings. During these events Helen Duncan would be tied to a chair and wear only a loose-fitting dress with no undergarments. She would be examined by female spiritualists to ensure that there was no cheating. It all seemed foolproof. However, on 3 May 1933, her world fell apart when Helen found herself on trial at Edinburgh Sheriff Court on charges of receiving money under false pretences by, 'pretending that she was a medium through whom spirits of deceased persons were openly materialised to become visible to and converse with those present in the room with her.' In other words, she was being accused of being nothing more than a fake. The trial, which attracted journalists from around the globe, and for which individuals from across the UK were called as witnesses, gives a fascinating glimpse into the world of Edinburgh mystics of that era.

Helen Duncan was living at 1, Wauchope Place, Niddrie Mains, at the time, but the seance, for which Helen had been booked as the medium, and which subsequently led to her trial, had been held at 24, Stafford Street on the evening of 5 January 1933. The seance took place in a room on the top floor of the house, a corner having been partitioned off by curtains as a cabinet for the medium. Inside the cabinet a chair was placed for Helen to sit on. Before the seance began the main lights

*Spiritualists attending a séance at which psychic mediums
contact phantoms of the dead.*

were switched off so that the room was illuminated solely by a
dim, red, 40-watt electric light. A candle flickered in the background. In the room there was also a 120-watt, unlit electric
hand lamp, which was to play a key part in the events that
followed. Helen entered the cabinet and curtains were then
drawn around her so that she could not be seen. Meanwhile,
the sitters arranged themselves in a semicircle in front of the
cabinet to await the spirit presence. The candle was put out so
that only the red light shone and the audience started to sing
as this was believed to encourage the spirits to 'come
through'.

After a little more than two minutes the voice of 'Albert'
was heard. He was Helen's 'spirit guide' and well known for

cracking jokes and making risqué (at the time) comments. To the sitters he joked, 'That is an awful voice you have for singing, Miss Maule. If you heard what it sounds like you would not sing again.' The room erupted in laughter. Other voices were now heard, including that of 'Little Peggy', a child spirit who was frequently 'brought over' by Helen. Several apparitions then materialised glowing white in the darkened room.

It's not clear whether the seance was set up deliberately to discredit Helen or if members of the audience became suspicious. However, Miss Maule who owned the house suddenly grabbed the figure of 'Little Peggy', who had by now appeared outside the seance cabinet as a white phantom. She told the trial that as she took hold of the 'spirit' she realised that 'it was no more than an object made of soft material' which tore as 'Little Peggy' struggled to break free. Miss Maule then pushed the curtains apart while another sitter Miss Mackay switched on the powerful hand lamp. They claimed that they discovered Helen bending forward, clearly not in a trance, stuffing a white object inside her top. Helen refused a request to show what it was she was trying to hide, but eventually agreed to strip if all the men were asked to leave, which they did. She then removed her clothes and a white stockinette vest with a hole in it fell to the floor. To the charge that this was the object she had been waving about, pretending that it was the spirit of 'Little Peggy', Helen replied evasively, 'It might have been. I'll no' say no.' On the surface her response appeared incriminating and led to criminal charges being brought against her.

During the trial, although there was a feeling that Helen had 'let the side down', many spiritualists stepped forward to support her. A doctor, Mary Hutchinson of King's Park, Glasgow, told of a test that she had put Helen through. She had been stripped naked to ensure that she was not concealing anything on her person then given only a black shift to wear which had been inspected thoroughly. However, even under these strict controls Helen still managed to produce, from her mouth and other orifices, a vast quantity of the mysterious substance called ectoplasm; a thick white material which, while it is floating through the air, is used by spirits to form a 'body' so that they can appear in human form in our world. The volume of ectoplasm Helen produced covered an area of twelve square feet. As Dr Hutchinson told the court:

> Nobody who had undergone the examination Mrs Duncan underwent could have concealed such a quantity about her person. Mrs Duncan had the assistance of some power which I cannot explain and could produce phenomena which it was impossible to produce by sleight of hand.

Evidence was given by sitters at Helen's seances of the wonderful sights they had witnessed; communication with long-dead loved ones and even the sight of them 'in the flesh' as they materialised in seance rooms. Even so the case went against her and Helen was fined £10.

So was Helen Duncan a fraud? There is no doubt that psychics, like anyone else, may feel pressurised to produce results when, on occasion, they may be unable to. People who visited her desperately wanted some contact with their relatives on the 'other side'. Helen may have, on occasion, tried too hard to please. But if she was nothing more than a cheat how did she manage to relate the sinking of *HMS Barham*, a wartime state secret? And why did a government, in the middle of a World War, set out to gaol her if they did not take her psychic abilities seriously? There is evidence that, even after the war was won, police and the security services kept tabs on Helen. Surely there is no stronger accolade to her psychic abilities than that.

Though Helen was a medium of ability, arguably she did not match up to the weird powers of Daniel Home. However, the city seems to be linked inextricably to those of a mystical bent, producing many psychics of repute. So did Edinburgh also produce the greatest physical medium of the twentieth and twenty-first centuries? Normally, when we think of a psychic, we assume that they are making contact with the spirits of those who have passed into another world. But could these 'other worlds' include those populated by beings we would not consider human? And how does this link in with the life of a famous film star? In fact, does contact with the spirit world provide the best proof that alien entities really do exist?

In February 1995, I received a strange phone call. I had been involved in investigating a number of UFO sightings, which had been covered in the local papers. As a result I had been contacted by many people all of whom had some strange incident they wanted to tell me about. But this call was very different. The voice at the end of the line asked me an astounding question: 'Do you want to see an alien?' At this point I might have put the phone down. I was used to people phoning me with extravagant claims, but this topped them all. So why didn't I simply say 'no thanks,' put it down to a hoax call and forget it? I didn't believe for one moment that I would really see an alien, but I did wonder what had motivated the man to make him sound so unusually convincing. And that was how I first came to meet Ray Tod.

Tod, as it turned out, though almost unknown to the general public, certainly ranks as one of Scotland's leading mystics and most powerful mediums. I and others did 'see' an alien, but that was only a fraction of strange events that unravelled in the unlikely setting of Ray's sparely furnished living room. And the man, small, overweight, balding and existing on a limited income was an unlikely figure as a medium. However, he never once asked for money and though he could have earned a living from his amazing abilities he was anxious to stay out of the limelight, inviting only a select group of individuals to witness the bizarre events that he was capable of producing. For over two years, I and others visited Ray Tod and participated in dozens of seances where he acted as the medium. The results were astonishing and experienced by so many people that it is hard to conclude that each one of us was either being deluded or the victim of an over-active imagination. Tod's dearest wish was that he could be tested by an organisation like Edinburgh University's 'Koestler Parapsychology Unit', but unfortunately he died before that came to pass.

Ray Tod lived in a second-floor, rented flat in West Montgomery Street, a few minutes from Leith Walk. The living room in which the seances took place was rather shabbily furnished, but stood out from the ordinary because of a range of stuffed animals and other objects linked to Africa, with which Ray felt a strong affinity. It lent the room an exotic air. Tod was a good talker and it was often difficult to get a word in, but he would listen and explain and certainly knew a vast amount about spiritualism and spirit contact. He was very matter-of-fact about the bizarre events that took place, especially considering that he was the channel of it all. He often passed on comments that he said the spirits had made to him. One, which he repeated frequently, ran, 'You think you're investigating us, but who do you think you're kidding? We're investigating you.' Ray found this amusing, but there was a disturbing aspect to such comments. I often wondered just who, or what, were these entities Ray appeared to be in touch with?

Anyone whose experience of a seance has come from books, films or television would be surprised at those held at Ray Tod's flat. In the first place, the spirits appeared through Ray in conditions of full light. It's true that these took place in the evening and, on occasions, on darker nights when the sun set early, but all the lights in Tod's living room were switched on at all times. Not I, nor anyone else who had a sitting with Ray, ever had a 'dark room' seance. There was no area of Ray's person which was not fully illuminated by light.

So what did the sitters glimpse at a seance with Ray? An incredible number of spirit faces, as clear as day. Phantoms of those who had lived at one time, but were now, Ray told us, resident in another world. The faces that appeared could be seen in full detail including beards, hair styles and glasses. I can only describe it by comparing it to watching a series of film clips running before your eyes, except that they were not images from fiction, if one could believe one's own senses but the actual spectres of those who had passed over and were now visiting from the spirit world. They would appear in rapid succession, one after the other, as if in a rush to reveal themselves.

In terms of 'seeing an alien' Ray did not disappoint me. The seance I attended on 24 May 1995 was certainly a memorable one as on this occasion I did see the face of an 'alien'. I described it shortly after as:

> a puffy-faced alien. The face was light grey, round shaped with what seemed like tubes running from the back of the head in a circular shape to the nape of the neck. The most prominent aspect, however, was the eyes [which had] no proper eyeball in the sense that we would recognise. I did get the feeling, however, that he (or she?) was staring at me. The head was completely bald, or, at least, looked extremely smooth. The face was very lined.

I admit that I found this experience disturbing. If the spirits of 'aliens' were 'coming through' what did this say about the spirit world or mankind's place in the universe? However, the 'aliens' were a minor aspect of the many sights I witnessed. These were, to borrow a phrase, definitely 'seances in the raw'; seances at which physical changes appeared to take place in the physical body of the medium and in the surroundings in which we were sitting.

At this seance, however, an event occurred which threw me and I have puzzled over ever since as it did throw into question the nature of what Ray Tod was doing and what I was seeing. A succession of faces followed that of the alien and then, completely unexpectedly, the face of Richard Todd appeared. Faces could appear incredibly clearly and there was no doubt that this was the same actor who appeared in the memorable 1950s' film *The Dam Busters* among others. But in 1995 Todd was very much alive and did not die till December 2009, at the age of 90. I have never managed to solve this enigma and the fact that a living person's face should appear among so many deceased ones has raised concerns in my mind over what was happening. However, against that is the fact that many people who attended Ray's seances saw these spirit faces as clearly as if they had been sitting next to someone on a bus and, in many cases, on comparing notes, the same phantoms had appeared to each one of us on separate occasions. Could all of us over several years and on many visits have been imagining these incidents? I have no doubt that 'something' was going on though people may, understandably, come to differing conclusions.

A seance would start with Ray chatting. After a while — and the length of time varied — sitters would notice a change come over Ray's face. It seemed as if it was dissolving and some kind of thicker material was forming over it. Then, incredibly, other people's faces would start to appear very clearly and distinctly. Normally, these were not, I should explain, faces of people that

I recognised or knew. Nor were they faces of famous people from the past, with the odd exception.

Although the format of the seances did not change in any way, each one produced varied results. The same spirit faces appeared from time to time, but many appeared only once. A fellow investigator, Bill Adam, acted as a compiler of notes at the seances. The description of what took place is taken directly from the details he typed up, from notes supplied by the participants.

Andy Smith described a seance he attended on 21 March 1995.

> We started the evening by chatting for a while. During this time I had the distinct impression that faces were forming. Eventually Ray went into a 'trance'. The first face that appeared was a surly looking person I had seen before. Faces then emerged quick and fast. The bald-headed gentleman, quite severe and haughty looking. I'm sure I caught sight of my grandfather. There was a man with fair, short-cut, frizzy hair. These figures all looked normal. Then came the monocled person, who Ray later explained was the doorkeeper. He was the 'spirit' who protected Ray during a seance and decided who to 'let through'. According to Ray he was his most important contact. All psychics require some form of protection from the 'other world'. In Ray's case this was doubly so as he, as a physical medium, was allowing spirit entities to use his body to 'come over' from the spirit world. That this had an impact on Ray, both physically and mentally, I have absolutely no doubt.

Jim Edgar attended a seance with Ray Tod on 10 March 1996. You can sense the amazement as he wrote down what he had observed.

At one point an Egyptian face appeared. It was broad and round, but the most striking point was the straight black hair. I immediately identified it with the pictures of ancient Egyptians seen constructing the pyramids. Ray's right hand was glowing as if there was a pink force field or aura forming a duplicate hand beside his own. The living room kept moving around until I felt quite dizzy. I had noticed this effect on previous occasions, but this time it seemed especially noticeable. The whole shape of the room appeared to change. The door seemed to come in at right angles to where we were sitting so that it was parallel to our chairs. From beneath the door at floor level an intense streak of light could be seen. I have not witnessed this before. Overall, the whole room looked to have shrunk to about a third of its size and it felt claustrophobic.

After the seance was over Tod would ask the sitters to describe who or 'what' had 'come through'. The paradox was that these phantoms were appearing in his sitting room, but as they were using his body to materialise, he could not see them himself. I found this aspect unsettling as not all the spirits who appeared seemed by any means friendly and some looked, I have to admit, downright hostile. I mentioned this to Ray who, however, took it all in his stride convinced that his spirit friends would look after him. Tod refused to make money from his amazing ability. 'I don't want to be turned into a freak show', he explained to me.

Edinburgh has produced many individuals who though interested in the realms of the supernatural don't set out to contact entities from other worlds. From the 1960s to his death, Charles Cameron was a well-known Edinburgh psychic investigator who built up a large library of artefacts and books on the occult. He was also a curator of the capital's 'Wax Museum'. He did an enormous amount to bring to public attention the variety of paranormal phenomenon that was taking place in and around the city, and was the first to name Edinburgh as the country's supernatural 'hot spot'. It's not clear to what extent Charles Cameron claimed psychic ability, but he certainly did have a number of experiences. He told of the night when alone in the 'Wax Museum', formerly a children's shelter, he was walking on the top floor when his torch suddenly failed. He found himself stranded in the pitch black with no one else in the building. It was an unnerving experience which, as he fumbled for the exit, became frightening when all around him he sensed the presence of children standing and whispering to each other. It concentrated his mind wonderfully and he managed to make a quick get-away. Having found myself in similar circumstances in a haunted building I, for one, certainly know how he must have felt!

Cameron did not see the paranormal as 'supernatural'. According to his view, 'Everything, whether it be ghosts, death by sorcery or even fortune-telling by tarot cards all occur strictly according to natural laws.' What Charles Cameron was suggesting was that as the 'paranormal' was subject to laws then it must be possible not only to access these events readily, but also, in effect, to control them. He believed in the power of 'magically charged talisman and medieval curses and witchcraft.' He had no doubt that an individual may, on occasion, be able to affect matter through the power of the mind, as modern physics indeed suggest. Cameron was ahead of his time in the way that he realised psychic powers could be abused. In the early 1980s, when the public was less aware of the British and US Governments' experiments with psychics and their potential for use against an enemy, Cameron argued that a 'psychic war' was possible. He went a step further suggesting that gifts to a foreign leader could be charged magically with a ritual incantation which would affect the mind of the person receiving the present. Is there any evidence that this has been done? Not that I'm aware of, but given the secretive nature of governments, and what we have learned of the many bizarre attempts by the CIA to assassinate the Cuban leader Fidel Castro during the 1960s, one could hardly doubt that such a scenario might well have occurred or might even be planned at this moment.

It would certainly seem that an area such as Edinburgh possessing an 'other wordly' aura might encourage the development of the mystical side of even the most hard-headed type. It was after taking up the post of Astronomer Royal of Scotland in Edinburgh that the English-born Charles Piazzi Smyth started to' go off the rails' as his colleagues saw it. Smyth, who lived between 1818 and 1900, is the founding father of Pyramidology; the belief that the measurements incorporated within the Great Pyramid at Giza posses both a mystical significance and a hidden message. He wrote several lengthy books detailing his research on the matter in which he argued, among many other 'facts', that the whole of human history had been documented in the angles and lengths the builders had used to erect the pyramid. By working out the numbers involved and their relationship to each other all significant dates in Man's past could be known and his future forseen. When his scientific colleagues scoffed at his discoveries Smyth abandoned astronomy. But his ideas spawned a long line of successors and his belief, that the Great Pyramid hides a myriad of secrets just waiting to be revealed, is more popular today than ever.

Even those with a natural talent find that a visit to the capital encourages psychic visions. In the 1980s, Highland Seer Swein Macdonald, who was often referred to as the contemporary Brahan Seer, was visiting the city. I met Swein in the 1990s at his Highland home. He was a big bear of a man with flowing hair and huge hands. He insisted on hugging all and sundry and you feared that a bone or two might be crushed in the process! But for all that he was an amazing psychic. I learned of a visit he had made to Edinburgh where he experienced an astonishing revelation. As he was sitting with friends in a restaurant the conversation turned to the disappearance of five-year-old Caroline Hogg who had last been seen in the garden of her Portobello home. Suddenly it was as if Swein had been taken to another place. He sat upright and banged his fist hard against the tabletop three times in rapid succession. He then told his startled friends that he had seen Caroline lying dead in long grass in a lay-by. This turned out to be accurate. It was eventually discovered that Caroline was a victim of the child killer Robert Black. However, Swein, who had a voice to match his presence, had been overheard by several people and his prediction was reported to the police. Such are the dangers of possessing the ability to see events others can't. At one time, no doubt, Swein would have found himself destined for the bonfire reserved for witches and those of similar bent.

The dividing line between the mystic who becomes a saint and the one who finds himself condemned is a fine one. In another age, Edinburgh's Margaret Sinclair might have faced an uncertain fate. Instead she is one of the very few Scots who may be raised to the sainthood. Margaret died as far back as 1925 when only in her mid-twenties, but many miraculous cures have been reported by people who have prayed to her for help when suffering from a life-threatening condition. It is even said that she made a blind person see again. Celebrity Jimmy Saville has claimed that it was through Margaret's help that his life was saved when, as a two year old, he suffered a bad fall and was seriously ill. His mother, apparently, found a prayer card about Margaret in Leeds Cathedral and asked her to intervene. Shortly thereafter, the toddler's health improved rapidly. Margaret Sinclair's body now lies in Mount Vernon cemetery. It would be remarkable if this daughter of the city, a former factory worker at McVitie's who died at such a young age, were to become Scotland's first female saint for several centuries.

Margaret, though she may reach a pinnacle denied to others, must be seen as part of a wider phenomenon that often lies hidden. Edinburgh abounds with psychics, many of whom are regularly found in spiritualist churches and other venues across the city. Several have worldwide reputations. In the 1990s, I interviewed spiritual healer Bob Cook. He assured me that 'everyone can heal. We've lost the ability over the years. We've become too civilised'. Maybe Bob was right, but perhaps the aura that surrounds the city, that unknown quantity which seems to attract the paranormal, has also led Edinburgh to breed more than its fair share of those who posses that mystic power which, for want of a better word, we label 'psychic'.

6

Ghost Capital

If there is one aspect of the paranormal that is most closely linked to the streets and wynds of Edinburgh then it must be that of the ghost or phantom. Certainly, the capital is an ancient site and castles and crumbling ruins, not to mention age-old graveyards, appear as natural spots for encountering spirits of the dead. But why should hauntings occur in more modern locations? In pubs, cinemas or clubs? Even in such a recent building as the new Scottish parliament? In 2009, hearing reports of strange incidents taking place there, I offered to investigate the alleged haunting. I was not surprised at this news having forecast before the building was put up that the site would be subject to powerful energy forces, which would produce weird effects.

I had dowsed the site during the building's construction and had discovered that streams of energy were flowing across the area. At the time I was looking at this in the context of the potential effect on MSPs and their decision-making. It hadn't occurred to me that this might allow spirits of the past to invade the building. In fact this is just what appears to have happened. As far back as 1707, the year the old Scottish parliament was dissolved and united with England's, a gruesome murder took place in the kitchens of the mansion house owned by the Duke of Queensberry in the Canongate. The area where this killing took place now forms part of the Scottish Parliament complex and is occupied by the office dealing with MSPs' allowances and expenses. What makes the story even more horrific is the claim that a young lad was put to death there in a gruesome manner, being roasted alive on a spit. That may be a detail too far, but there's no doubt that a murder has been linked to this site and that may explain the recent incidents that have disturbed staff who work there. These have included unexplained noises and the aroma of roasting meat. I have also been told of sightings of a young boy, late at night, who gradually fades away as he walks along the corridor, but I have been unable to verify these incidents.

Without more research into events it is difficult to establish exact details. I offered to investigate the area in a non-obtrusive manner, including a questionnaire to relevant staff, a procedure I had used successfully elsewhere, but unfortunately my attempts to look into the matter met with resistance and I was denied access. However, the incidents do show that a ghost may linger for a long time and that the re-building of a site can somehow cause a disturbance which may reactivate the phantom of the long dead.

However, ghosts should not simply be seen as things of the past. These phantoms appear among us today, so we can say with certainty that they are all around us and with us as we go about our daily business. And though some appear as spirits of the deceased from past eras others may have a far more recent pedigree.

In 1996, the 'PJ Lyles' pub in Leith Walk was the site of a series of strange occurrences. Staff were disturbed by a range of weird noises heard when no one else was present in the building. There were various odd incidents. Glasses and other objects were moved around after they had been left overnight. The landlady, Elaine, suspected that the spirit of a dead 'regular' had been upset by changes that had been made to the pub. Events came to a head one weekend, as Elaine explained: 'On Friday a few of us were clearing up and we heard footsteps running across the ceiling above us.' This on its own was peculiar, but what was truly disturbing was that the footsteps did not come to a halt and carried on as if whatever was making them had run right through the wall. Incident piled on incident. One Sunday the police called the assistant manager to the pub as the burglar alarm was ringing. On its own this was not an unusual event, but when he got there curtains over the windows upstairs had been pulled down and pot plants and other items had been thrown on to the floor. It was as if someone had stormed through the building in a mad frenzy. However, following an examination of the premises it was clear that no one had, in fact, broken into the pub and it was as securely locked as it had been the night before. It was a mystery and one which unnerved staff to such an extent that several said that they wouldn't work there again, till whatever was behind the strange incidents was gone.

Pubs do seem to attract ghosts, although given the number of drinking outlets that are on the go at any one time I would argue that phantoms are no more likely to appear there than elsewhere. When it does happen it just seems to attract media interest. Be that as it may, several bizarre cases of ghost activity have been linked to pubs within the city. In December 1986, events at the Hunter's Tryst Inn at Oxgangs attracted considerable attention and were investigated by journalist Rab McNeil, who wrote an account of the events. The assistant manageress, Rena, reported that she had actually seen the phantom said to be haunting the place. She recalled:

It was like a mist, but you could see the figure. She seemed young, but as she had her back to me I couldn't actually see

Haunted 'Hunter's Tryst' long time scene of ghostly events.

her face. She had a long blue dress on with a bustle at the back, and she wore a small crinoline sort of cap. She just floated down the restaurant. I was in the kitchen at the time and I saw her move towards the coffee lounge. There was nothing said. I wasn't frightened. There was nothing evil about it at all.

The Hunter's Tryst appears to have existed as long ago as the 1740s and was a popular meeting place for Edinburgh citizens as, at the time, it lay well outside the city's boundary and a visit there was on a par with taking a ramble in the countryside. Interestingly, it also had a reputation as a haunted spot. As far back as the 1870s, at a time when the building had been converted into a farmhouse, it was alleged that it suffered from the presence of a strange entity. The being appeared to have no good intentions and was described as the 'Devil' or 'Satan'.

Reports of the incidents suggest that, during this phase at least, the phenomena resembled more that of poltergeist activity rather than a true haunting. The whole building would shake while groans and shrieks echoed through the rooms. Plates were thrown around and smashed to the floor in the early hours of the morning while the family slept. An unearthly staccato of drumbeats would travel up and down the roof. Attempts were made to exorcise the demon by ministers of the Kirk, but they were not successful and the poltergeist continued to be active. Eventually, however, true to the pattern of behaviour of this 'spirit' the disturbance stopped by itself.

Events reported in the 1980s, however, did not repeat those of a century before, though there was little doubt among those who worked there that 'something' was still present at the Hunter's Tryst. Shortly after she started working there, the manageress, Marilyn, became aware that there was a different 'aura' than that usually found in a pub:

> I felt there was definitely something in the place. The atmosphere would go cold. One Sunday I locked up and took my two dogs out for a walk. Suddenly, when I looked back, the whole place lit up like a Christmas tree. I checked the burglar alarm. It was still working, but it hadn't gone off.

Other members of staff, past and present, were convinced that there was an eerie atmosphere and felt nervous about locking up at night on their own. Several confirmed that after they had closed the inn and turned all the lights off, they would come back on as soon as they walked away from the premises. Staff denied that this could be put down to an electrical fault and believed that something more sinister was at work. A friend of those who worked there, Mike, described what had happened on one occasion:

The bar was closed and I was waiting for [a member of staff]. The light had been left on in the coffee lounge. Because of the room's ghostly reputation the barmaids were not keen to go and switch off the light. So I went. I found the temperature dramatically reduced in the room. It was not a fault in the heating or anything like that. It was something totally different. A kind of cold. It made the hairs on the back of my head stand on end. I switched the light off, then came back down the unlit corridor. The light in the room came back on again. I was startled. I asked the girls if they had switched the light on from the bar as a joke. But they said it wasn't possible. I eventually persuaded myself to go back and put the light off again. This time, as far as I remember, it stayed off.

Mike added, 'The incident I experienced certainly can't be explained by an electrical fault.'

It's undoubtedly true that most ghosts are witnessed inside an enclosed space, but there are many reports of phantoms encountered in a street or on open ground. Why should this be? Several apparitions have been witnessed along Constitution Street. One is of an elderly lady in an old-fashioned dress clutching a posy. Normally, she has been seen in the evening walking from the direction of Coatfield Lane and fading as she turns the corner of Queen Charlotte Street. A number of witnesses have claimed to have encountered a man in Highland rig-out running down the centre of the road at the dead of night and simply disappearing, as if he had vanished into a black hole.

An explanation for the frequent sightings of ghosts in Constitution Street emerged with the excavations carried out by archaeologists as roads were being dug up in preparation for the city's new tram lines. It appears that when Constitution

Street was constructed in 1790, it was built over part of the cemetery that once adjoined the old South Leith Parish Church. Archaeologists estimated that around 300 bodies lay beneath the then new street. It is well known by psychics that the disturbance of a graveyard in this way can lead to the phantoms of some of the dead appearing in the area, although the reason for this is obscure. It will be interesting to see if, over the next few years, there is an increase in sightings of ghosts and similar entities.

However things develop in Consitution Street, it may be a while before it reaches the level of events in the 'Old Town'. The Royal Mile is well known as the place where a spectre might be encountered and the activity of spirits of the dead shows no sign of quietening down. In September 1998, I was contacted by a witness who reported a strange incident he had experienced. Jim wrote:

> About two weekends ago I came down the Canongate at about 1 p.m. I stopped at Calton Road intending to cross. I glanced to my left looking for traffic. There was no traffic coming, but I had a glimpse of a young woman who appeared to be looking up Calton Road towards the East End. She was wearing a long brown dress with a hood, which was down on her shoulders. Her dress was tied in the middle with what looked like piping, with the ends hanging down the front. My impression was that she was standing between a window and a door. I thought she was in fancy dress. I intended to have a better look after I had checked for traffic. I looked back to my left and she was gone. The street was empty. There was nowhere for her to go. I realised I had seen a ghost. I have been back to the site and there is, indeed, the shape of a window on the wall of the cemetery. The door I 'thought' I saw is not there.

*South Leith Parish Church on Constitution Street. Has digging
up the road alongside, once the site of a cemetery, disturbed
the spirits of the long dead?*

Jim enclosed a drawing of the woman he had seen and, if the
style of dress is anything to go by, then she certainly looks as
if she could be the phantom of a lady from the fifteenth century.
Those familiar with the city's geography will realise that Jim's
encounter took place close to the Scottish Parliament site and
Holyrood; an area which is particularly prone to paranormal
influences.

However, in at least one instance, a phantom in the street
was captured on camera. Every investigator has been looking
for the ghost photo that will prove the phenomenon is real and
not a mere figment of the imagination. One of the most puzzling
was caught by David Knott early one morning in August 1987.
He was taking snaps of the Old Town including the Royal Mile.

He wanted to make sure that he could get photographs of the buildings without people in the way and that was why he was out and about in the 'wee hours'. However, when David developed the film he had shot he was surprised to see a strange looking figure standing on the pavement at Castle Hill. He was certain that there had been no one there when he had taken the photo as he had made sure the area was completely deserted. At first glance, the figure looked like a woman dressed in a black shroud. Closer examination, however, revealed what appeared to be a man's head emerging from the shroud. The figure, when compared to the height of a window in the wall behind, was no more than three feet tall. There are possible explanations for some aspects of the photo. If it is a ghost then it may be that two apparitions were photographed who are bonded together in, and therefore appear together from the spirit world. On the other hand, it is often reported that spirits seem to be walking at a level lower than the present day, which may reflect the lie of the ground at the time they died. In this case, there's little doubt that the street levels have changed significantly over the years and this could explain why the phantom appeared to be small, as the lower part of its body was hidden beneath the level of the pavement and could not be seen.

There are some places more than others where you might expect to encounter a ghost. Hospitals are one such spot and though incidents do occur they do not appear to be as frequent as might be expected. Or, perhaps, doctors and nurses are simply less likely to report such an encounter, in the same way that airline pilots are reluctant to report UFO sightings for fear of questions being raised about their competence. In the early 1970s, Ellen was working as a night-duty nurse at the Western General. As she walked back to the ward where her patients were she saw, coming towards her, an elderly looking woman,

*Do phantoms from the city's distant past still haunt the
Royal Mile? Drawing of a ghost encountered by a witness
in the Canongate.*

wearing a nightdress, which immediately struck Ellen as being
rather old-fashioned even for mature women of the time.
However, her main concern was to get the lady back to bed as
there was no reason for her to be in this part of the hospital.
She was about to ask her which ward she had come from when
she was horror-struck to notice that the woman's legs had
disappeared through the floor. Paralysed as a thousand thoughts
ran through her mind Ellen stared as the lady kept on walking
towards her and then passed right through her body. It was
an experience which traumatised her for some considerable
time.

A staff nurse working at a different city hospital was another who got a shock while on night duty. She was alone in a high-dependency room checking that everything was in order to receive a patient. Suddenly she became aware of a presence and glancing at the bed saw a man lying there with a tube inserted in his throat. The vision then faded before her eyes.

It's often said that children are more aware than adults of the presence of phantoms. On a ward a defibrillator machine kept switching itself on and off. At the same time as this was happening staff kept seeing a child wearing old-fashioned striped pyjamas wandering around. They ordered him back to bed repeatedly only to discover eventually that the 'patient' didn't exist. It was an apparition of some kind. Meanwhile the 'defib' machine kept acting up. As it was doing so one night, and staff were trying to sort it out, a young patient, Andrew, came over and said, 'Billy! Stop playing with the machine!' Immediately it went off. Andrew told the nurses that he had been watching 'Billy', a boy in striped pyjamas, playing with it.

The dead, or some of them at least, appear determined to hang on to us. Mary King's Close has earned a reputation as a hotbed of ghostly activity although it is not clear why this should be the case. It was, allegedly, shut down after an outbreak of bubonic plague in the seventeenth century with the implication that many died here or, more brutally, were left to die in agony from the effects of this deadly bacterium. The site was eventually re-opened as ground was needed to house a growing population and so, in 1685, Thomas Coltheart moved in with his wife to a smart new flat. He was shortly to regret it. One afternoon, feeling unwell, Coltheart lay in his bed with his wife sitting beside him, reading to him. Suddenly, she became aware of an object to the left of her and, turning around, was confronted by the sight of a head, with no body, hanging in mid-air. Even worse was the fact that the eyes seemed alive and were staring straight at her. Mrs Coltheart fainted.

It seems that Thomas had not seen the phantom head at this point so it may have vanished immediately after his wife's encounter. However, that night, soon after he had gone to bed, the head appeared again and, as in his wife's case, the eyes kept staring directly at him. Coltheart's prayers for help went unanswered and he could not make the apparition go away. The gateway to another world had, for whatever reason, been well and truly opened. The head was next joined by the phantom of a child which also hung in mid-space and, bizarrely, by an arm which, in the manner of a clip from a horror film, attempted to shake Coltheart's hand. But that wasn't all. The apparition of a dog appeared, followed by a cat and what are described as 'other and stranger creatures'. These entities swarmed all over the floor. It must have appeared like a vision out of hell. And then suddenly it was all over. Coltheart prayed again for relief and, whether it was coincidence or not, there was a sudden noise resembling a groan and all the spirit intruders disappeared in a flash.

Coltheart, apparently, stayed in the house and there is a strange postscript to the events. On the night some years later when he passed away, a close friend staying in Tranent was woken by the family nurse who had been disturbed by the appearance of what looked like a cloud whirling round the room. The cloud gradually condensed and as it did so it took on the shape of a man; a man they recognised as Thomas Coltheart. The phantom was asked if he was indeed Thomas and why he had appeared to them. According to the account, 'The ghost held up his hand three times, shaking it towards them and vanished'. If Thomas had a message to impart the content was not clear. But it certainly gives the impression that it was a warning of some kind. Coltheart's friend rushed over to Mary King's Close to learn that Thomas was indeed dead.

Not so far from here, at a spot on Castle Hill, once stood

the palace of Mary of Guise, the French-born wife of King James V. The palace itself was demolished as long ago as 1845, but before then the premises had been split into apartments and rented to families. A prized remnant of its one-time glory was an oak-panelled door that, in one of the flats, separated the bedroom from a linked smaller room. But this apartment was also haunted. Several family members reported hearing the slow but deliberate footsteps of a man coming up the stairs then approaching the bedroom door. The door did not open, but the phantom came right through it. He looked old, but wore a distinctive green coat with two yellow buttons on the back, and yellow trousers. Research later revealed that the clothes matched the livery of Mary of Guise's household and it was even suggested that this could be the outfit of her court jester. Those who saw the phenomenon testified that the apparition looked as solid as you or I, but passed right through the ancient oak door before disappearing.

But if the door was somehow linked to the appearance of the ghost, is there any proof that anything happened after the palace was pulled down? There is some evidence to suggest that this was indeed the case. As a relic of Mary of Guise's time in the city, the door became the property of the Museum of Antiquities. I have been told that on a number of occasions a figure, wearing brightly coloured clothes, was seen mounting the stairs in the Queen Street building and then disappearing. Was this the same spectre? It's hard to be sure without more evidence or being certain of the ancient door's location. However, spirits it seems can become as attached to particular objects as any of the living.

We can, of course, too readily assume that when a phantom is seen we are dealing with a spirit of a dead person. Some incidents, however, suggest that this is not always the case and do raise some issues over just what we are dealing with. In 1991,

Mary was sitting in the living room of her bungalow in Blackhall. There had been nothing out of the ordinary during the day, nor was there any crisis that she was aware of to distract her from the 101 things that a woman juggles to make sure that a household runs properly. In fact, as she relaxed in the armchair she was thinking about nothing in particular. Suddenly, she became aware of her daughter sitting in the chair opposite. Not as a phantom, but as solid as a real person. Mary sat up startled. Her daughter lived hundreds of miles away in Paris, so what on earth was she doing in the house? And how had she got there? Mary, having recovered, from the shock, was about to say something when her daughter started to dissolve in front of her eyes and simply disappeared. This was even more disturbing and Mary didn't know what to make of it. She knew that Christine was alive and well, but the horrible thought struck her that maybe something had happened to her and she had, in classic fashion, been visited by her ghost. She immediately got on the phone to Paris and was hugely relieved to hear her daughter's voice on the line. She was alive and well, but she did have some emotional news to impart. She and her husband had decided to separate. It had been a desperately trying time and she had struggled to come to terms with telling her mother. So had this emotional conflict somehow generated a doppelganger to warn Mary of the crisis taking place hundreds of miles away?

Sometimes apparitions can be confusing. What are we dealing with? An angel from heaven? A spirit of the dead? A messenger from another world? In February 1978, a woman was renting a cottage in East Lothian. Out of the blue something happened which was to drastically change her view of the world. As she recalled:

Around a quarter to seven in the morning I was woken by a warm sensation all over my body. I opened my eyes and I saw rays of exceptionally bright light though it didn't hurt my eyes. Within seconds an image started to appear. A woman with long, blonde, shoulder length hair, an aquiline nose, very soft looking skin with a glow, wearing a long satin silky robe down to her feet with a blue sash. On the feet were gold sandals and a rose on the toes. All the time the apparition was there I felt a great warmth through my body almost like a heavenly feeling of great comfort. I felt totally relaxed. I was overcome with joy. I cannot find words to describe it exactly. The rays of light coming out from the head of the vision lasted throughout the sighting. It gradually faded away altogether.

This encounter appears to have been an almost pleasurable experience, if that is an appropriate word for the presence of a phantom. Other incidents strike you as rather more poignant. In 2006, Des, a former engineer, described an event he had experienced some years before when he had been visiting friends at a Stockbridge flat. He told me:

We'd had a late night as we hadn't seen each other for a couple of years even though we'd been good friends, having met when we were all at Edinburgh Uni. I went to bed in the early hours expecting to get to sleep as by then I was feeling drowsy and I'd had a fair bit to drink. However, I found I couldn't drop off which, at first, I put down to the fact that I was in a strange bed in a strange room. Then I began to wonder. I had the sensation that there was 'something' in the atmosphere of the room that was stopping me getting off to sleep. It was now about 3 a.m. and I had been lying with my eyes shut for ages though still awake. It was then that I heard the sounds of someone crying very softly and I knew straight away it was a child. My friends did not have any children, but this was quite clearly coming from within the room I was in as it was getting louder as it came nearer the bed. Then the foot of the bed sank down as if a person had sat on it. I immediately looked up in surprise and I saw a little girl in pyjamas sitting there at the end of the bed. I'd guess she was maybe ten or eleven years old. She was sobbing. I don't doubt what I saw as there was a bright aura surrounding her and everything stood out clearly even to the dark fringe of her hair that fell down one cheek. I was then shocked to notice bloodstains across her pyjama top. I'd been more fascinated than terrified up to that point, but, I admit, the sight of that made me jump out of bed and utter an army type exclamation. The girl then disappeared. I turned on the light and had a good look around, but nothing. I didn't sleep much after that. I agonised over whether to mention it to my friends, but, curiosity got the better of me and I decided that I would. They, as it turned out, were a bit embarrassed saying that another friend had seen something in the room, but as they themselves hadn't had any similar experience in the two years they had been there, and others had slept there with no problems, thought she was simply imagining it. They had heard of no rumours or stories about anything having happened in the flat so could not explain what lay behind the little girl's appearance. I tried a bit of research, but I have been unable to discover any event that would account for it.

Sometimes ghosts seem to haunt a place for a while then just disappear. A house on Craigmillar Park in Newington was visited by the same apparition for several years, but has never, apparently, been seen since. Those who saw him described him as a small, grey-haired man with rounded shoulders, invariably wearing a dressing gown tightly tied round the middle with a cord. The house where the events took place was over 100 years old so there had been plenty of time, you might guess, for a variety of residents to have lived there, died there and to have become very attached to it. Margaret, who owned the house and who described the series of incidents, glimpsed the apparition in the summer of 1914, just before World War I began. She was in the dining room making a frock when she suddenly felt a cold breeze which lifted her hair high above her head. Startled, Margaret looked up and caught sight of a small man walk through the main door, which was lying open, then stand beside the staircase. Wondering who he was and why he had come in unannounced she stopped what she was doing and walked quickly into the hall, only to discover that there was no one there. She couldn't explain it as there was no way that the man could have got away without her being aware of it. He had simply vanished.

A few years later, Margaret was sitting upstairs in the drawing room which was, as it happened, situated directly above the room where she had been when the earlier experience occurred. At around midnight she decided to go downstairs to pick up a few things. As she did so she saw the same man standing in the identical spot at the bottom of the stairs where she had first seen him. As she watched he disappeared before her eyes. Margaret saw him on one more occasion, some time later in 1923. She was lying in her bedroom, which was located on the ground floor, when she awoke suddenly at around about two in the morning. A strange urge which she couldn't explain led her to open the bedroom door. As she did so she saw the man again walking through the hall. He seemed to disappear into the wall. She never saw him again.

Margaret did not feel frightened by the spectre's appearance and, indeed, felt that every time she saw him something pleasant tended to happen. It has to be said that this is an unusual experience as the sighting of a ghost has tended to be thought of as the harbinger of bad news. But, even though she did not find his appearance disturbing, she was curious to know who the phantom might be. Eventually, she was told by a long-standing resident in the area that the house had, at one time, been occupied by an individual whose appearance fitted her description of the apparition. However, there is no way of knowing whether this was accurate or simply shoe-horning an explanation into the event. It would, however, be in keeping with what psychics say about ghosts, that some of them do not wish to leave a place where they have had happy memories or some tragedy has taken place. It would be interesting to learn whether the same phantom had ever re-appeared. However, domestic residences can only be investigated by invitation when the owners are willing to allow investigators in. Other buildings, less personal and unoccupied, however, offer a fascination of their own. The ghost phenomenon can more easily be researched at such sites.

On 3 October 1998, together with members of the Scottish Earth Mysteries Research group, I entered the Niddry Street Vaults just before midnight having been given permission by Mercat Tours to stay there overnight. The area occupied by the 'Vaults' was at one time the location, during the eighteenth century, of various shops and apartments. When the South Bridge was erected the 'Vaults' area was built over though the shops were left as open premises. They became derelict and eventually abandoned. However, the empty shells of the shops, their walls and windows intact, can still be visited down a long flight of stairs inside a dark and dingy subterranean cavern. You will then find yourself within this long-forgotten shopping arcade. Forgotten? Not by the phantoms of those who once worked there it seems and there have been many reports of ghosts sighted and strange events witnessed.

Accompanying me on this investigation were Brian Wilson and psychic medium, Katrina McNab, among others. Katrina quickly identified several of what are known as 'cold spots'.

*Entrance to Niddry Vaults: site of the legendary 'underground city'.
'Ghostbusters' have experienced 'cold spots', phantoms and
spirit faces here.*

Cold spots are, as the name suggests, areas where the temperature is much lower than the surrounding air. They are often linked with the appearance of a ghost. Odd incidents then started to happen. Brian Wilson noted that:

Ron tried to make vocal notes on his Dictaphone, but complained that he could not get it to work. He tried several times to tape his notes, but it just would not respond. Only when coming out of the room did the Dictaphone work and this startled us. Ron

144

went back into the room and again the machine would not work. Then when he came back out into the hall suddenly it started to work again.

I remember thinking at the time that the refusal of the device to work in that area was truly odd and I was glad that there were people present to confirm it as I would not have believed it myself. I normally had no problem with it whatsoever and it did start working when I moved away from that particular area so what caused it to malfunction was a mystery. As Brian wrote we 'felt the hairs on our head stand on end.'

As we wandered down the central street with the various rooms, the former shops, on either side of us, Katrina sensed the atmosphere thicken and become more dense. She complained of feeling sick. As we walked into the remains of the old workshops Katrina identified one where jewellery was made and the place where a butcher's once stood, as she experienced an overwhelming sensation of blood flowing. Having, after an hour or so, completed our initial look round we decided to locate ourselves in the larger room and got ready to set up the video equipment. We had three video cameras with us, but were startled to discover that the first video camera would not work. Surprised, we set up the second. That wouldn't work either. Was it simply coincidence? We had brought a third camera. That refused to work too and when we attempted to eject a tape from the camera nothing happened. We were extremely frustrated at this point as the cameras were a key part of the night's investigation. Katrina informed us that the spirits present were playing a trick on us and that there was nothing that we could do about it ourselves.

This did, indeed, seem to be the case. After we had sat around disconsolately for half an hour one of the cameras suddenly started to work again, out of the blue. As we now had only one camera operational we agreed to focus it on Katrina as she appeared to be in strong communication with the spirits. She told us that 'a hooded priest or holy man was sitting watching us at the top left-hand corner of the room and that he was telling her that he had come here centuries ago when someone was dying and gave them the last rites.' As Katrina was in contact with the spirits a face, like that of a man smoking, appeared on the wall behind and at an angle to where she was sitting. This could be clearly seen on the video clip. In fact, several strange features had been recorded, but this only became clear later. We left the Vaults in the early hours of 4 October and, to our surprise, but not to Katrina's, the two video cameras immediately started to work. It was hard to fathom it all.

We had taken around thirty photographs. This, of course, was in pre-digital days and when we had a chance to look at these the results were astonishing. Brian recalls:

> There was one photo which really got my attention. It was the picture of the hallway where there appeared to be two alien type faces/skulls on the photo. I then scanned this into my computer and started to blow up the picture. It convinced me even more that this was definitely not a trick of the brickwork. I went back into the Vaults to check the brickwork and where the alien faces are there were no bricks at all, but a gap in the side wall. This convinced me that light or background walls played no part in the image. It was so convincing that the *Evening News* had a look at it and analysed it, then published it.

Individuals who suspect that a ghost has invaded their home often look to an investigator to confirm that what is happening is not simply down to their imagination. In December 1995, I visited a modern house near the Royal Mile where, the occupant felt, there had been some paranormal disturbance.

Judith explained to me the background to the events, which she believed could not be accounted for by any normal explanation. She told me that her mother had died over a year before of a serious illness in the house where she, Judith, lived. She had in fact, met her death in the sitting room, where we were meeting at that moment. Judith told me that she could sense her mother's presence and felt sudden drops in temperatures which coincided with the 'arrival' of her mother. She confirmed that she could not see her, but was aware of her being there with her. Judith's son confirmed that he too sensed his granny in the house. A curious fact, Judith added, was that the neighbour's dog would not come into the sitting room although before her mother's death it would wander in without any problem. It's an often reported fact that animals appear to have a sixth sense for detecting phantoms from the spirit world.

Judith told me of a range of other odd events which had occurred following her mum's death. A month after she died the front door had opened then shut on its own. Since then the sitting room door, and other doors, would open and close for no apparent reason, but it seemed to coincide with the presence of her mother's spirit. As in many cases of haunting the spirit seemed to link to one specific area and that was the sitting room, but she seemed to come at no particular hour and Judith sensed her presence at a variety of times during the day. Sometimes she was aware of her being there because she could smell the scent her mother used to wear. There was a chair in the room close to Judith's own and she felt that her mother's spirit would often sit down there beside her. There were aspects to the case which you might have expected, but weren't present. No objects had been moved and, apart from doors being opened by an invisible hand, there was no other clear physical manifestation of a ghost's presence. Nor had Judith or her son been aware of any coloured balls of light or anything resembling that phenomenon which often indicates that the spirit of a dead person is present. However, a spirit appearance can take many forms and we might expect that a mother, having passed to the 'beyond,' would be likely to make her presence felt to those she was close to in life.

Shortly after her mother died Mary was standing at the kitchen sink washing up some dishes in her home at East Restalrig. She was thinking about nothing in particular, but was suddenly disturbed by a voice whispering 'Mary' in her ear. She spun round expecting to find someone behind her, but the kitchen was empty. She could, however, sense a presence although of whom she could not say. Nor could she recognise the voice that had called her name. There was one odd thing though. Her dog would at times run to the top of the stairs and look down as if he was aware of someone coming up the stairs though when Mary went to look there would be no one there.

However, it is clear that things other than personal affection attract phantoms of the dead. It is said that no true actor can resist a curtain call. And that, it seems, applies to ghosts as well. Edinburgh's 'Theatre Royal' once stood in Shakespeare Square. The strange events that took place there were reported by the Jackson family who, at the end of the eighteenth century, lived in a flat above the theatre. Apparently, once the regular performance was over and the building had been shut for the night strange noises could be heard coming from the auditorium. It was the sounds of movement and the echo of voices as if the plays performed there for a living public were being repeated again by a cast of apparitions for a truly phantom audience. Those who went in when they heard these sounds claimed to see figures flitting across the stage, but which would disappear immediately like a will-o'-the-wisp.

It's not clear who the ghosts involved in this instance might have been, but in the case of the Festival Theatre it is claimed that the apparition seen there in recent years is that of a famous performer. On 9 May 1911, Sigmund Neuburgher, who used the stage name the 'Great Lafayette' and had a reputation as a leading magician of the time, died when fire broke out in the Empire Theatre, Nicolson Street, during his act. He was buried in Piershill cemetery. What might seem more natural than the

Burial place of the 'Great Lafayette' – does the ghost of the famous actor still haunt the stage of the Festival Theatre where he was killed by fire in 1911?

spirit of such a legendary performer seeking to return to the stage, especially to the very one where he played his final curtain? However, no known sightings of the spirit of Lafayette were made till the 1990s, by which time the 'Empire' had been reconstructed and re-emerged as the 'Festival Theatre'. The age of the 'Great Lafayette' was only a distant memory. He, however, had most definitely not been forgotten so when a tall, dark apparition was encountered backstage, at the spot where it is said the fire began back in May 1911, it was identified immediately as that of Lafayette. Several sightings then followed including that of a figure, around six feet tall, gliding though the stalls. I have also been told of a phantom wrapped in a dark cloak, arms outspread, having been seen on the stage itself after the theatre had closed and the audience and most staff had left. Lafayette playing to empty seats? It seems out of character and it might be wondered if we really are dealing with the ghost of the great performer. Given the fleeting sightings and the time that has elapsed since his tragic death, it is hard to be definite about who this might be. On the other hand, the fact that he did die in terrible circumstances at this spot does suggest that he has a strong link to the theatre. It also has to be remembered that the sightings took place after the theatre was renovated and, as is often the case, changing a building does seem to stir up the spirits of those connected to it. This may well explain why Lafayette reappeared after such a long gap in time.

Almost every theatre in the city, past and present, seems to have a ghostly association. The Royal Lyceum has been visited by a phantom 'blue lady' seen, apparently, in a gallery. The figure waves a hand before vanishing into the ether. It has been suggested that this could be the apparition of the nineteenth-century actress Ellen Terry, perhaps better known these days as the secret, long-standing mistress of Charles Dickens. A chalk statue of her, it is said, used to stand in the theatre's foyer. However, the link between the ghost and Terry may be no more than speculation. There are several instances of theatre phantoms being recognised as the spirits of those who once worked there, as has been suggested may be the case of a ghost encountered at the Playhouse Theatre. There have been reports, stretching back many years, that the building is haunted. Incidents have included alarms going off when no one is in the building, lights switching on by themselves, unexplained cold spots and sightings of a hazy figure. No famous actor, however, has been put forward as the dead spirit behind these events. It is said that a night watchman hanged himself in the 1950s, in the building, and his troubled spectre could still be present doing his rounds as he did in life. However, it is also rumoured that a stage technician who died in an accident behind the scenes, but who loved his job, might be the phantom reluctant to leave the place he loved so much. It's said that he was a bit of a practical joker and might still enjoy playing games with those in the land of the living.

More recently, in 2007, Bill White experienced a strange encounter in the King's Theatre at Tollcross. Bill was anxious to assure me that he was not a natural believer in the paranormal and was a 'down to earth' type. In fact his job in IT might suggest, he joked, that he was a bit of a 'nerd'. 'What happened', he told me, 'came right out of the blue.'

We're not avid theatre goers, but we do like to see a play from time to time. On this occasion, when the interval came, my wife decided to nip to the loo while I went to the bar to order drinks as there can be a bit of a queue. Sue was going to join me as soon as she could. I'd been there several times so thought I knew my way, but this time for some reason I got lost. It seems odd given the number of people about but I suddenly found myself on my own heading up a flight of stairs. I was going up and up and then the stairs simply came to a dead end against a solid wall. The realisation hit me that I had obviously gone the wrong way. I cursed myself for being stupid and thinking I'd maybe not have enough time to get the drinks in, so I started to go back down as quick as I could. It was then that I saw it. It happened so quickly that it was over before I realised what had happened. A woman, and I'm sure it was a woman, came up the stairs towards me. But she was floating above the level of the steps. One part of my mind reeled in shock and the other part refused to believe it. She was wearing old-fashioned style clothes that's all I can say as the next second she had passed by me and literally disappeared into the wall. I have never moved so fast down a set of stairs in my life. When at last I got to the bar Sue was there and asked me — rather indignantly — where I had been and what the matter was. She could see I was not my usually calm self. When I told her, she didn't believe me at first. I could hardly believe it myself. After the play finished we went to see if we could find the stairs again. But we drew a blank. I felt too awkward to ask staff about it. But I've wondered if anyone else had seen the same thing.

In my experience theatres appear to generate more ghosts than cinemas do, though I'm not sure why that should be the case. Could it be because they tend to be older, or because theatres are populated by actors and not simply the images of those who are broadcast on the silver screen? In the 1960s, I was a regular attendee at a cinema called the 'Poole's Synod Hall'; a rather dilapidated building which stood on Castle Terrace to the rear of the Usher Hall. It was demolished a long time ago and the site stood empty and unused for many years. However, before then it was a real magnet for those who loved watching horror films. It was in the days when films deemed suitable for those over eighteen were X-rated, but staff at Poole's were never too fussy about how old you were and, provided you appeared approximately in your teens, you would be let in. It was a tense moment though as you asked for a ticket wondering if you would be refused admission. I was there many times, but had no psychic encounter of any kind. However, many years later, while investigating a haunting in another part of the city I met Rob and learnt that he had once worked at Poole's. He told me that in his view the building had definitely been haunted, though patrons might not have been aware of it as incidents tended to happen when the place was empty. He said that at times it could be quite unsettling. On one occasion he was clearing rubbish upstairs when, behind him, he heard seats suddenly banging down as if someone was sitting on them. He knew the seats could not do it by themselves as they were on a spring mechanism. So, when he turned round to look, he expected to see someone there, but the seats were empty. Mystified, though not unduly disturbed thinking there must be an obvious explanation, he went to take a look. He had almost reached the row when the seats shot back up again one after another with a distinct thud. Next he heard seats bang down close to the spot where he had been working just the moment before. Glancing round he noticed that a kind of haze seemed to be building up at the edge of the balcony. Rob admitted that he lost his cool and left as quickly as possible. 'I was edgy working there on my own after that', he admitted.

However, if odd things happen at your place of work you at least have the security of knowing that it is possible to escape the attention of the dead. It's a different matter when you are forced to experience it in your own home. By the 1990s, a family had been living in their flat beside the Meadows for nearly forty years. The woman, Ella, who had bought it, was aware before she had moved in that a man had committed suicide in the area that she now used as her bedroom. He had hung himself by a noose suspended from the ceiling. That could explain, she had guessed, why the price had been reduced to a level at which she could afford to buy it. However, in some ways, there was a cost to pay. The spirit of the suicide seemed determined to maintain contact with the site of his death and the family could not escape his presence. As Susan, Ella's daughter, told me:

> I saw a face, a man's face, pure white floating through the kitchen door. My mum went into the bedroom where my dad was in bed as he had been feeling unwell. The phantom was there too. My mum got such a fright that she shouted out 'go away' and threw her arm out. It went straight through it. We didn't like it, but we just lived with it. Another time, a friend, Andy, was in the house and saw a man going up the stairs with Jesus-type sandals on. He just disappeared.

However, perhaps it wasn't simply a question of a suicide haunting the place where he had met his end. Maybe there was an aura about the flat which somehow allowed the spirits of the dead to make their presence felt, as other events suggest? Tragically, Susan's brother, Bill, died at a comparatively early age. On the day of the funeral Ella, feeling the pressure of it all, was lying on the bed. As Susan described it, 'She heard someone open the back door and then walk in. She got up to see who it was and saw Bill standing on the stairs. "I'm all right" was all he said and then disappeared.' Interestingly, there appears to have been physical effects of the presence of 'something'. On a number of occasions Ella heard noises in the back room and when she went to investigate found condensation on the window, as if someone had been standing there looking out — something that Bill, apparently, used to do. A few incidents, however, bordered on those associated with a poltergeist. From time to time, Susan felt a pressure on her stomach, as if something was pressing down on her and a round white circular indentation would appear. On one occasion she was thrown across her bedroom by an invisible force. However, unlike the determined poltergeist presence these incidents were exceptional and did not turn into a series of events.

It is difficult to understand why ghosts appear on some occasions and not on others. And why they visit some individuals, though many, if not most of us, pass through life without ever encountering a phantom from the 'other side'. However, few will deny that Edinburgh, and especially its heart in the 'Old Town', is a place where ghosts, in all their varied guises, seem more willing than anywhere else to present themselves. And even in the twenty-first century these 'visits' show no sign of dying out. Quite the opposite, in fact.

7

Phantoms of the Sky?

UFOs hovering over Princes Street? Alien beings abducting people from moving vehicles? Can such events really be taking place in and around Scotland's capital city? In November 1993, at 5.20 p.m. Sheena Williamson, daughter of 'Flower of Scotland' composer Roy Williamson, was walking along Princes Street, on the shop side heading for the Caledonian hotel. Sheena explained what happened next:

> Suddenly I saw a ball of fire flying through the black night sky at a speed so fast that I shrieked and took hold of my son's hand as I pointed it out. This ball of fire was going faster than any aeroplane or meteor or satellite. I kept thinking it would explode or disappear but it just kept travelling in a level and very straight direction. I lost sight of it as it went over the roofs of the shops I was standing beside. It seemed to come from the south and be heading north. There was no sound with it otherwise I would have thought it was simply one of those fast jets the air force use, but even those aren't fast enough for a comparison with what I saw.

What is so strange, but so typical of Sheena's experience, is that though the incident happened in the busiest of streets no one else came forward who claimed to have witnessed the event. But that, surprisingly, is the norm. UFO sightings tend to have few witnesses no matter where they take place, which does raise a question over the exact nature of what is being seen. Is it a psychic experience? Or is it a window into another dimension which opens so briefly that only the fortunate observer will catch sight of it? Whatever the explanation, encounters from across the city would surely convince even the most sceptical that something strange is going on in the skies above us, and may also allow us to draw a conclusion as to exactly what that 'something' is.

Sightings in the city have a lengthy pedigree. As far back as the 1940s, a witness caught sight of a strange craft hovering over the seaside district of Portobello. At the time Andrew Cherry was a twenty-two year old employed at a bottle works situated in the area. This, the first ever UFO encounter known to have taken place in the city, happened at 5.30 a.m. in July 1947, while Mr Cheery was standing at a bus stop in Baileyfield Road. In the sky he glimpsed a disc-shaped object with what appeared to be a large glass dome on top. The disc looked as if it was made of metal of a 'rough diamond' texture. But perhaps strangest of all was the fact that, as the UFO was hovering only three hundred feet above him, Andrew could see 'someone' or 'something' inside the glass dome. This 'alien pilot' wore dark-coloured clothes and was either standing or sitting beside what seemed to be a control panel. The UFO must have been powered by an internal fuel supply as flames were escaping from one side and, at the same time, Andrew could hear a steady humming sound. The area surrounding the object appeared hazy which could have been the result of heat from the power source. The UFO, which was about fifteen feet long, suddenly tilted then disappeared towards the Fife coast in a matter of seconds.

Strangely, the area around Portobello has continued to be a hot spot with several bizarre encounters. In October 1992, Pat Macleod, a policemen's wife, was driving along Duddingston Park at around 9.50 a.m. making for the local health centre in Mountcastle Drive to keep an appointment. As Pat drove she became aware of an extremely bright flashing light in the sky. Half a mile further on, keeping the light in view, she realised it was getting bigger and the brightness intensifying. In fact it was drawing much closer to her and as it approached she noted that the central sphere of light had a ring, or flange, round it. This reminded Pat of pictures she had seen of the planet Saturn.

At about twenty to thirty feet from the ground the object slowed down and appeared to hover. She could see now just how large the UFO was, which she judged to be about the length of an aircraft wingspan. At regular intervals around the circumference Pat noted squares of light which resembled glowing windows. Pat continued her journey, arriving at the health centre shortly after 10 o'clock, but as she drove she was still able to observe the object. She had turned off the main road down a side street and watched as the UFO veered east, in the opposite direction from her, and gradually descended. It appeared to land in an area of open ground called Niddrie Burn, a valley-shaped expanse of grass with a stream running through the centre. Although this is open land it is surrounded by multi-storey flats. Oddly, not a person came forward to admit to having seen the object. Nor did anyone driving on the road at this time step up as a witness. Pat, however, took the encounter so seriously that she called the police to find out if anyone else had seen the UFO. No one had, but Jon Jeromsom, who ran a plumbing business in Duddingston Park reported that he had been looking out of his showroom window when he saw a bright object descend to around fifty feet from the ground. It hovered for several seconds and then vanished. As this incident took place at 10 a.m., around the same time as Pat's encounter, it could well have been the same object though the descriptions don't match exactly. It's curious too that the encounter with a half-bird half-man creature occurred in this area; an incident dealt with elsewhere in the book. Was there a connection between these two events? It's possible, though there may be, as I suggest, another potential explanation.

There's no obvious answer to the puzzle of why UFOs would be attracted to a particular area, but only a few years later Ann, from her home in Niddrie, reported seeing a hovering disc-shaped object. On 7 June 1995, she woke up in the early hours noting on her bedside clock that it was 2.15 a.m. As Ann described it, 'for some reason I was drawn to the bedroom window where I drew back the curtains.' Ann's flat was on the third floor so she had a good view across the city skyline. Her attention was caught by 'a slow-moving very low-flying object approaching from the east.' She watched it come towards her and gradually realised that 'something wasn't quite right.' The object was 'flying far too low and didn't have any wings. In other words it wasn't a plane.'

The object passed Anne's window about a hundred yards away and only forty-five feet from the ground. It then hovered over the houses opposite her block. She judged it to be about thirty feet across with intense bright red and white lights. The lights, Ann indicated, were a striking feature, especially the red light which she said was enormous; so big that she could actually see inside it and thought that she caught sight of something moving around. The encounter lasted a total of fifteen minutes so Ann had some time to observe the UFO. The picture she drew shows a round object with a rim, red and white lights underneath and a bowl-shaped structure above the rim with what appear to be porthole type windows. It has to be acknowledged that there is continuous traffic into the city airport through the night and there would certainly have been a plane in the sky at around this time. However, it also has to be agreed that Ann had a very good sighting of the object which hovered within feet of her window. It was the very fact that it was not behaving like a plane and was flying so low, that convinced her that she was experiencing something quite out of the ordinary.

Sightings of objects which look for all the world as if they are 'spacecraft' may, on the surface, appear to have no direct connection to those experienced by witnesses just a few miles away in Musselburgh. But, some have suggested that there is, in fact, a link, bizarre though that may seem. In the winter of 1981, Mr and Mrs Buckley were walking along the pavement opposite the race track when they spotted an object which they described as being like a brilliant white tennis ball. The 'ball' was hovering beside a lamppost about twenty feet up and, at first, the couple weren't sure exactly what they were seeing, but then it moved. The couple could now observe that there were two balls moving close together and coming towards them. The couple were struck by the intense brilliance of the balls, 'a fierce white colour' and like 'metal boiling hot.' The balls had descended to about an inch from the pavement and then moved in front of the couple as they continued down the street. To Mr and Mrs Buckley it seemed as if 'the balls had a mind of their own' and that they were 'playing a game with us.' Intriguingly, one ball gave the impression of being 'more domi-nant than the other.'

Intelligent spheres of light the size of a tennis ball? Is there a connection between the nuts-and-bolts UFOs that we have come to accept as the indicators of an alien presence? Mr and Mrs Buckley did not see anything inside these glowing balls, and certainly no alien presence. But that has not been the experience elsewhere. In Australia, the 'Min Min' lights around Lake Manchester near Brisbane, in Queensland, are seen regularly. They are glowing balls of light similar to those encountered in Musselburgh, but with one difference. Small alien entities have been observed inside these objects. In his book *Earthlights,* writer Paul Devereux describes how one witness confronted by an eight-inch ball of light was stunned to see, 'a tiny, human-like entity inside the sphere. The being was bald, sitting cross-legged with its elbows resting on its knees and was staring intently at the witness.' There have been several reports similar to that, but not from Edinburgh, nor from Scotland that I'm aware of. But the city has experienced many incidents of glowing balls of light, especially over the Pentland Hills. Could there be some connection to the wider UFO phenomenon? Witnesses in the capital of alien entities have not described encountering such miniature creatures, but given the vast nature of the universe it has to be wondered if anything can be ruled out.

It's curious that Bob Taylor in his famous encounter on Dechmont Law, on 9 November 1979, described the circular object he saw as not wholly solid as he could see through it to the foliage behind. Bob was a sixty-one-year-old forestry worker for Livingston Development Corporation who, while doing his rounds, came across a strange object hovering, most likely, a few inches above the ground in a clearing in the woods on Dechmont Law. As Bob watched, two spiky balls, like World War II sea mines, emerged from the UFO, rolled across the grass and got hold of Bob's trousers. He was aware of a pungent smell then passed out. It is not clear how long Bob was unconscious, although at least twenty minutes is the general view, but when he came to and raised the alarm a police investigation followed. No satisfactory conclusion was arrived at to explain what had happened to Bob and it remains one of the most convincing cases in proving the reality of an alien presence. In 1992, I with support from other ufologists persuaded Livingston Development Corporation to erect a cairn and plaque to mark the site and I have been campaigning for a more fitting memorial to this remarkable event. Although it took place some miles outside the city it's close enough to provide powerful evidence that backs up sightings of strange objects seen over the capital. And these objects, according to some, may be located in underground bases in the hills surrounding Edinburgh.

But why is it that UFOs appear to be attracted to specific objects and locations? In 1962, thirty-two-year-old Charles Farquharson was training to be a teacher at Moray House College. He travelled there on a daily basis from an address in South Queensferry, close to the Forth Railway Bridge. On the day in question he arrived home at around 4.40 p.m. and as there was no one in he decided to make himself a cup of coffee. Charles recalled that 'it was a lovely clear evening.' It was so nice that he walked over to the kitchen window to look down the Firth as he had done many times before, never failing to be impressed by the scenery. But this time something unexpected happened. Next to the railway bridge he saw what he described as a 'flying saucer.' It was hovering slightly above the bridge at the highest part of the central span. Mr Farquharson judged that it was about thirty feet above the bridge and the same distance to the side. The UFO appeared to be quite still and tilted about twenty-five degrees from the vertical. Charles felt that he could get a good estimate of these distances because the object was close to the bridge and so he had something to compare it to. In addition, Charles had been so intrigued by the sighting that he moved into the garden and stood on the surrounding wall to get a better look. He, therefore, judged the craft to be about twenty feet across. The UFO stayed in position for a quarter of an hour before moving very slowly in a

The Forth Railway Bridge – site of many UFO incidents.
Could there be a secret alien base located near here?

northwards direction, following the line of the railway. It stayed
in his line of sight for a further four minutes disappearing in
the direction of Cardenden, in Fife. During his observation of
the object David noted that it had 'no features of any kind
which interrupted its symmetry.' The colour he described as
like 'a new penny, burnished cupronickel.' Charles was
convinced that the UFO had been studying the bridge's
construction and, possibly, the rail network in the area. But
was it all imagination or even a mirage? He is convinced it was
not and with good reason. The witness has an engineering
degree and so was in a good position to give a view of the
technical qualities of the object seen.

There is one more telling point. UFOs have been spotted

frequently in the area, so Charles's sighting was by no means a one-off event. In August 1997, several UFOs were seen hovering over the Firth of Forth. Derek Davis was videoing the night skies over the Forth when a circle of bright light caught his attention. He was sure it wasn't a plane or other natural object as he filmed these at the same time and they did not look anything like it. The object was motionless for several seconds then suddenly disappeared. But a more spectacular sighting had occurred on the 7 October 1990. It was actually the centenary of the opening of the Forth Bridge and the event was being celebrated by a firework display. Was it this what attracted an unidentified object? At around 9.15 p.m. Lyn Livingston, who was watching the display, caught sight of a circular object whose base was made up of intermittent red, blue and white lights. The UFO rotated and twinkled and, as it did so, it appeared to change shape forming a projecting cone of white-coloured lights. The object stayed in position for a full fifteen minutes before, as with the UFO witnessed by David Carter, it drifted towards the Fife coast. The evidence suggests that in both cases the objects had come from the south, that is, from behind the witnesses' observation point as they were looking north. So why did they stop at the Forth Bridge? One possible answer may be in the experience of Angela who claimed to have had an encounter with humanoid entities while travelling on a train which was crossing the bridge. According to her account, the entities which confronted her explained that they lived in tunnels beneath the Forth Estuary. They did not indicate, however, why they were based there or whether their occupation had any wider purpose.

This sounds undeniably bizarre, but does link with my investigation into other UFO cases in the Edinburgh area and my reassessment of the Burry Man, the festival of uncertain origin that takes place annually in August, in South Queensferry. On the first Friday, one of the villagers dresses up in a strange costume. He is encased from head to foot in a cloth to which have been sown thousands of burr pods. His head is covered by a helmet also covered in burrs except for a small opening for his eyes and mouth. The Burry Man finds it very difficult to move in this outfit and struggles around like one of those clips you see of men walking on the moon. It takes little leap of imagination to link the Burry Man to some wild imitation of a modern astronaut. And before you think it a leap too far it will come as a surprise to learn, perhaps, that similarly dressed figures appear in ceremonies across the world to which are linked tales of visitors from distant planets.

The Kayapo Indians of the Upper Amazon in Brazil have an annual ceremony to mark a strange event. The leading men in the village wrap themselves in suits made from straw. On their heads and necks they place a helmet also made of straw. They are, in fact, completely enclosed from head to foot in this odd garment. As they move around with an awkward shambling gait they undoubtedly resemble the film of astronauts stumbling across the lunar landscape. And, bizarre as it may appear, this is exactly what the Kayapo Indians are commemorating by this ceremony; a visit by a being who claimed to come from the skies. According to their legend one day there was a massive explosion of earth and fire on a nearby hill. Out of the fire came a being that they attacked with spears, but their weapons simply bounced off the gleaming white suit the entity was wearing. Eventually the Kayapo grew less frightened of the being and began to communicate with 'him'. According to their tradition, the visitor taught them to make medicines which cured the illnesses they had been forced to accept until then as an inevitable part of life. They called the stranger 'Bep Kororiti' which translates as 'I come from space'. One day the visitor left them, wearing the white suit he had on when he first arrived and disappeared in a blast of smoke and fire. As the Kayapo did not write there is no way of finding out when this incident occurred. However, given that these events were first recorded in 1952 and appear to have been part of the folklore for several generations it rules out any suggestion that someone from the earth visited them. However, what is of key interest is the similarity between the Kayapo festival and the Burry Man. Could there be some common memory of visits by extraterrestrials? One is entitled to be sceptical but yet there is a tantalising hint of something so strange that it appears to defy common sense. And though it may defy common sense, the fact remains that, across Edinburgh, individuals repeatedly claim sightings of objects that go by the description of 'spacecraft.'

In the 1950s, several strange incidents took place around the capital. Were these events connected? The first was serious enough to have the Edinburgh CID called in to investigate. This was a revelation to me as, until I researched this case, I had been under the impression that the only time that the police had been directly involved in investigating a UFO incident was the famous 1979 Bob Taylor UFO encounter at Dechmont. Mary was one of sixteen Edinburgh 'tattie howkers', twelve women and four men, returning home one Friday evening around 5 p.m. following a day's work at a nearby farm nursery. As the lorry they were travelling in drove along Hailes Road, between Musselburgh and the capital, a strange object suddenly swooped down from the sky. It flew behind the vehicle leaving in its wake two distinct vapour trails and followed them for about ten minutes. According to another witness, the UFO had lights on its underside which glowed as it moved along. Mary described an object about the size of a large dining-room table which had a dome both on top and underneath and was light grey in colour. Tony who was also on the lorry described 'a rim of flame around the ring' and a 'silvery green light coming from a small bubble underneath.' The UFO came so close to those on the lorry that they were forced to duck as it flew over them. Whatever the object was it created panic, with some of the group banging on the cab trying to get the driver's attention. Oddly, the driver did not see the UFO so ignored his passengers' frantic efforts. Family members confirmed that when members of the group returned home they appeared quite terrified by the incident. However, the UFO did not appear to have harmed anyone physically and suddenly shot back into the sky, headed towards the Firth of Forth and disappeared. It may have been the same UFO sighted around 5.30 p.m. in Anniesland in Glasgow by two ambulance men, but we can't be certain of that.

At around the same time, other odd incidents were reported of the kind which ufologists, rightly or wrongly, have linked to UFO sightings. The first of these was a report that the bodies of three dead domestic animals, pigs in this instance, had been seen floating in the River Almond in the Lothians. It may be argued that there is nothing remarkable in this, but what is odd is that the discovery of these carcasses led the police to conduct a search of the river. It's unclear, given the passage of time, just exactly what they were looking for, or if anything else strange was found. Over the years there have been reports of animals found in bizarre circumstances, as in a mutilated sheep discovered near Edinburgh airport, parts of which appeared to have been surgically cored out. Not long after this, in January 1958, there was a dramatic and unexpected rise in water consumption in the country areas surrounding the city which puzzled representatives of the water department. They eventually explained it rather feebly as individuals running off water to avoid taps freezing over. Although one can see the logic, it has to be asked how many households would it take to cause such a dramatic impact? And why then, and not before or since?

It has been reported worldwide that UFOs appear to hover over and be interested in water sources and especially reservoirs supplying drinking water to cities. And Edinburgh is no exception to such reported incidents. Although there are no known sightings over Edinburgh reservoirs that would coincide with the events of the 1950s, there certainly have been reports of UFOs seen at other times. In January 1997, a couple observed a bright ball of light which appeared to be hovering over the Hopes Reservoir in East Lothian. The object then changed shape and colour, flashing red, blue and purple lights. According to the witnesses the UFO was silent and made no noise. It did though appear to be emitting a shining light which lit up the surrounding area. After about an hour the hovering UFO disappeared as suddenly as it had arrived. Two years earlier, in September 1995, a witness, an ex-RAF man, observed an orange-coloured round object passing over Harlaw Reservoir. And it has also been noted by UFO buffs that the A70 abduction of Gary Wood and Colin Wright occurred near to Harperrig Reservoir. Sinister interpretations have been put on the interest of UFOs in our water supply, although some suggest it's used for their own purpose possibly as some kind of fuel propellant.

Are UFOs seen in the vicinity of key hills within, or fringing, the city heading there for equally sinister reasons? Blackford Hill has been the scene of several UFO sightings. As far back as October 1966, two school boys, Eric and Stephen, reported a strange object that they both caught sight of. Chatting in Gladstone Terrace around 8 p.m. they suddenly noticed what they described as 'a flying saucer' appear in the evening sky. They judged it to be around a half mile away when first seen and noted it was heading straight down in the direction of Blackford Hill. Both witnesses were sure the object was not a plane. They described it as having white, red and blue lights on top and a circle of lights around its base. Although it's not certain from the surviving evidence, the report seems to suggest that the object was disc-shaped. It's also not clear whether or not anyone else witnessed this event, which is puzzling when you consider that the UFO's lights were flashing and that flames were pouring out of a rounded tail area.

What is notable is just how much activity there was with regard to UFOs in Edinburgh in the 1950s and '60s, and the extent to which the capital took a spot on the world stage. As far back as January 1959, a Flying Saucer Club was formed by John Spark and, by April of the same year, the Scottish UFO Research Society as it was called had two branches, one in Edinburgh and a second in the Lothians. The society was actively involved in the visit of George Adamski to the city in May 1959. Adamski was visiting Britain from his home in the USA. Through his book, *Flying Saucers have landed*, co-written with Desmond Leslie, Adamski had gained world attention with his claims to have been contacted by visitors from outer space. Now he was in Edinburgh to repeat his claims. The year before, in February 1958, the city had been visited by another famous 'contactee', George King the founder of the Aetherius Society. King claimed that he had been given various secrets by alien visitors and repeated his claims at no less a venue than Edinburgh's Usher Hall. The *Scotsman* reported the event under the less than serious heading: INTER PLANETARY PARLIAMENT. THE VOICE ELECT SPEAKS OUT AT THE USHER HALL. Interest in UFOs reached such a pitch during this period that, on 17 January 1966, according to the Edinburgh *Evening News*, 'the first Scottish group of Sky Scouts' was set up at a meeting in Leith town hall. They had plenty to keep them busy. However, many years were to pass before Scotland was presented with its first publicised abduction case and clear evidence of an alien visitation.

On 17 August 1992, Gary Wood and Colin Wright set off from Edinburgh to go to a friend's house in the village of Tarbrax, fifteen miles outside the city. As Gary explained, 'The receiver on my satellite dish blew and I rang my friend Ian Phillips to see if he could help.' Gary's visit was not planned far in advance and as he was getting ready to go his pal Colin Wright turned up and decided to accompany Gary. It's interesting to speculate what might have happened had Gary left alone. It was around 10 p.m. that the pair set off judging that the journey should take no more than thirty minutes. The road they took was the A70 which, once it passes the villages of Currie and Balerno, enters an expanse of bleak moorland that stretches all the way along the lower slopes of the Pentland Hills to Carnwath. The small community of Tarbrax where Gary and Colin were heading lies off the main road at an isolated spot. As they drove towards Harperrig Reservoir, about five miles from Balerno, the car approached a blind bend. Colin Wright suddenly called out, 'What the hell is that?'

Looking skywards Gary caught sight of a large object hovering about twenty feet above the road. He later remembered it as being roughly thirty-five to forty feet across, black or dark-coloured and resembling a classic 'flying saucer' shape. It was windowless and looked as if it was made of metal of some kind.

Unnerved by the strange object Gary immediately hit the accelerator, aiming to drive underneath it and pull away as quickly as possible. As the car passed beneath it they were plunged into what Gary described as 'a void of blackness.' He also recalled a 'shimmering curtain' resembling the picture on an un-tuned television set descending around them and covering exactly the width of the road. In the darkness they felt something hit the back of the car. As Gary explained, 'And then I wasn't in the car. I was thinking, "Where's the car?"

"Where's Colin?" I could see only blackness and really thought I was dead. Then I was back in the car on the wrong side of the road with Colin screaming, "Did you see it?"' The object had disappeared and all they could make out was a starry sky.

Gary didn't hang around to investigate and drove rapidly, at speeds approaching 90mph according to Gary, to Tarbrax, where they found the house they were heading for in darkness. This was surprising as they knew their friends were expecting them. They had already experienced a strange journey, but now events were to enter the realm of the bizarre. They eventually roused their friends who had gone to bed. They had turned in because Gary and Colin had arrived at 12.45 a.m., nearly three hours after they had set out. A trip which should had taken no more than forty-five minutes had lasted almost four times as long. Both Gary and Colin were deeply puzzled. It seemed inexplicable. They had been together on a shared journey, but neither could find an answer to the puzzle.

Gary, however, soon started experiencing unpleasant symptoms including headaches and bouts of nervousness. He reasoned that there must be some connection with the events on the A70 on 17 August. But his mind could not come up with any direct link.

The mystery of what took place only came out when Gary underwent regression hypnosis; a practice intended to pull out from an individual's memory facts which are not recoverable by the everyday conscious mind and have, perhaps, been suppressed or hidden. A truly enigmatic story was revealed. Gary and Colin had been abducted from the car by alien enti-ties. They had been taken on board a craft of some kind by grey-coloured creatures which Gary described as having 'a translucent bone-shaped arm with long fingers.' Gary was kept on a hospital-like bed. From this spot he observed various incidents. In a hole in the floor of the craft, filled with some sort of sticky fluid, he saw 'a head appear out of it with a body and two arms.' He added, 'the creature must have been pretty big, bigger than me. It was like a skeleton with flesh around it. It had long arms, really long arms. It had a long body, really skinny, with the skin tight.' The entity had a large head with two prominent eyes, not of the human type, which were very dark. The flesh on its body appeared discoloured. It's interesting that in Gary's recall of these events the beings attempted and succeeded in communication with him not through speech, but by telepathy.

For weeks after, Gary suffered nightmares. One morning he found himself nearly a mile from his house, half dressed and dazed. Puzzled and worried, he tried to make sense of his encounter and why time was missing from his life. It was at this point that he decided to undergo hypnotic regression. Gary Wood described to me when I interviewed him in the 1990s the hidden memories that resurfaced:

> I felt I was in my car and it was like being electrocuted, as if my muscles were being pulled in on me. I saw three wee men coming towards the car. Then there was a taller entity, six to seven feet, translucent like a grey-white colour. It came close to me and said, 'I've got a life like yours, but different.' What it was trying to tell me was, 'look I'm not a monster.' There was also a brown-coloured being with a heart-shaped head and folds of skin about four feet high. It looked ancient.

From Gary's remembered account the entities also put him through a medical examination of some kind.

> I saw two objects go away from my chest. At the same time the entities were looking at my left leg. I couldn't move at all during

this time. There was an object right inside my ear making a humming noise.

One of the odd aspects of the incident was that Gary had no sight of Colin during these events although, given the experience related by other abductees, it would seem likely that they were separated and looked at in isolation. Gary, however, did see one other person. He described, 'a naked female on the ground, in her early twenties with blonde hair. She was trying to cover herself up. She was very distressed. Her eyes were red with crying.'

It's possible that the incident on the A70 was not Gary's first encounter as he had experienced a strange incident as a child. 'I went missing for most of the day when I was just four years old and where I was during all that time has never been explained. I just have vague memories of playing with children in strange-coloured sand.'

Interestingly, a month after the A70 incident, a witness, David, reported a sighting, on the other side of the Pentland Hills, directly opposite, as the crow flies, the spot where Gary and Colin experienced their encounter. On 19 September 1992, at 9 p.m., he was driving along an unclassified road towards Penicuik when he caught sight of a bright blue pulsating light moving low down over the Pentland Hills. It was travelling rapidly and David felt straightaway that it had glimpsed his car lights and was heading directly for him. Nevertheless, he stopped and got out of the car to get a better look. He was surprised to note that although he had not been aware of the light descending it had come down and now sat low over the moor. It wasn't clear to David just what the blue light could represent or what was going on, so after watching for a short time, and with no one else around, he decided to get away. But curiosity overcame him and he stopped by a cottage at a crossroads and looked back to where he had encountered the UFO. It could still be seen flashing quite clearly. The following day he returned to the scene to find out if he could explain the events, but there was no obvious answer and it remains a puzzle . . . but one in keeping with so many incidents reported from across the Pentlands.

The A70 abduction attracted considerable attention and, in Autumn 2009, there were claims in the press that the events were going to be turned into a film. Because of the use of hypnosis in extracting the memories of the witnesses it is certainly a controversial case. But against that the sheer volume of sightings in the Edinburgh area has to be considered. If these do represent an alien presence then the encounter experienced by Gary and Colin falls neatly into place.

And given the many witnesses to UFOs in the skies over the capital, can anyone seriously doubt that alien activity is a possible cause? At around 3.50 p.m. on Wednesday, 20 November 2002, several civil servants working on the fourth floor of the Department of Agriculture and Fisheries block in West Edinburgh saw a group of small objects moving rapidly and erratically over Arthur's Seat. The UFOs were observed for around twenty minutes until an aircraft, heading to land at the airport, appeared in view. At this point the UFOs shot upwards at high speed and disappeared.

At 8.20 a.m. on 30 November 1992, Mrs Lenzie was walking along the promenade with a friend beside Portobello beach when they spotted a strange object in the sky. It was rectangular in shape with four porthole-shaped windows with glowing lights visible. They watched it for a couple of minutes as it moved in the direction of Edinburgh. Could it have been a plane? As is often the case the witnesses had seen aircraft flying over many times and were convinced that this was something different.

At 4.30 p.m. on 16 December 1992, John, from his house in Leith, caught sight of a large bright object in the sky with lights suspended below it. He watched the object through binoculars for several minutes as it appeared to hover in the sky and did not move. It was then obscured by a cloud. The witness was adamant that this was not a star or planet. It's difficult to be sure given the restricted nature of the sighting. However, in one of those strange coincidences at exactly the same time and date, 4.30 p.m., Wednesday 16 December 1992, a witness in Balerno observed a blue light, which he described as 'electric' travelling over Balerno towards the Pentlands. Was there any connection between these two events, or was it simply pure coincidence?

On 22 May 1996, Peter saw a large white object which he described as 'misty-looking' and having a long protruding tail moving over Peffermill Road. The sightings took place at around 10.15 p.m. on what was a clear evening. The top of the tail was red and the underside orange. The object, though not very high above ground, travelled slowly across the sky for about a minute till it was obscured by a house and disappeared.

In December 1994, a woman driving near Prestonpans saw, in her rear-view mirror, a green ball of light travelling down the road behind her. It shot over the roof of the car at about the height of a house and accelerated into the sky. The lady was so surprised by this incident that she reported it to Air Traffic Control at Edinburgh airport. In response, they sent out what she described as 'an official looking form' to fill in; evidence that someone somewhere was taking these reports seriously.

In one case, a female witness was convinced that she had observed the same UFO on two separate occasions within a three-week period. The first sighting took place on Wednesday, 17 January 1996. The witness was waiting for a bus in Balgreen Road at around 5.30 p.m. when she saw what she described as 'a bright object' in the west. It hovered there for almost twenty-five minutes and appeared to be getting brighter as she watched. Then on Sunday, 4 February 1996, at 6 p.m., she was looking out of the window of her house in St Leonard's Street when she caught sight of the object again. On this occasion her partner was with her and was able to observe the object too. The suggestion that this might have been a planet or bright celestial body is contradicted by the fact that the male witness could make out four lights which appeared to be in a line. Two larger lights were on the outside and two smaller lights on the inside. As they watched the UFO, a plane took off which crossed beneath it, temporarily obscuring their view. After twenty minutes they ended their observation, but when they returned some time later the UFO had gone.

On Tuesday, 3 March 1997, Elaine was walking through the playground of Hopefield primary school in Bonnyrigg when her three-year-old daughter suddenly drew her attention to a strange object in the sky. Elaine looked up and was astonished to see what she called 'a big bright orange ball of flame' in the sky. It was trailing a plume of smoke behind it. The UFO stopped and appeared to hover. The event was dramatic enough to lead Elaine to go into the school to alert them to the situation, but when she came out the object had gone. Investigation afterwards led Edinburgh airport and the RAF to confirm that it was not one of their craft. So what on earth could it have been?

With the arrival of the twenty-first century, sightings of unexplained objects have continued with no apparent signs of slowing down. In February 2000, a 'bright oval object' was reported travelling at speed over Colinton and bizarre 'dancing lights' were seen over Leith in March 2001. Several years later, in December 2008, another witness in Leith glimpsed a pulsating orange light moving silently over the city. When, in 2007, the

Ministry of Defence issued its collection of UFO incidents for the area many similar incidents were listed, which at least proves that even the authorities are willing to admit that strange events are taking place in the skies over Edinburgh.

Witnesses to UFO incidents generally have only one encounter in a lifetime. But some people have several sightings and are known as 'repeater' witnesses. It's not clear why an individual should have more than one experience, but it may be that whatever UFOs are, they are active in the area where the repeater witness lives. Or, maybe the witness has some psychic awareness that allows them to see UFOs in a way that others can't. On 8 August 1996, Andrew McMichael woke up at 2.15 a.m. A fox had been coming into the garden and he was curious to see if it had eaten the food he'd left out for it. The plate had been licked clean, but as Andrew looked up he glimpsed something completely unexpected. He was, he told me:

> just in time to see an object move in an undulating path across the trees and houses at the edge of Frogston Road to the south of my house. It was completely silent and had a slight round bright red emission at the centre.

The UFO was oval in shape with a red dome. He estimated its size as around thirty feet long and fifteen feet from top to bottom. The object moved away in 'a slightly wavy pattern' then 'rose up as if to clear a clump of trees.' To Andrew it seemed to change direction twice, as though searching for something, before disappearing behind some sycamores bordering farmland.

This had been Andrew's second sighting of a strange object within a week. Andrew confirmed that on 2 August both he and his wife were woken in the early hours of the morning, at 3.15 a.m., by a dazzling white light. They both went to the window where they were almost blinded by an intense white light which was so powerful that they were unable to see outside the bedroom window. The light moved off silently in a westerly direction. Later, in conversation with neighbours, it emerged that others had witnessed this strange light and the sensation of an electrically charged atmosphere which Andrew had also felt in his bedroom at the time. However, his neighbours' sightings had taken place forty minutes after Andrew's which suggested that the UFO had been moving around the area for some time.

Some months later Andrew had further strange experiences which, on the surface, don't appear to make any sense, but could well have been related to these earlier events. On 23 December a large snowflake-shaped object, appeared on the bedroom window covering it completely. The following week a red swirling crimson dust appeared at the window blocking out the sky. When it eventually moved away the heavens appeared again.

Andrew's experiences, however, began twenty years before. In the late summer of 1976, at around 5.30 p.m., Andrew caught sight of what he took to be an aeroplane banking over Clermiston Hill. The 'plane' seemed to be moving in an odd way and Andrew caught his breath as it appeared as if it was going to hit a clump of trees on the hillside. Just as disaster seemed unavoidable the object flipped on to its edge to reveal a disc shape with a raised central area. The UFO was very large. According to Andrew, '300 feet across with a very elliptical profile and coloured blue and white.' Was this an attempt to camouflage itself against the background of the sky? The way it moved was also noticeably odd. 'Instead of moving as an aeroplane would, edge on to the airflow, the large disc moved upright, slowly at first, stopped, then just looked as if it switched off . . . or disappeared completely.' The area where Andrew had his sighting seems to be one which attracts strange events. Corstorphine Hill, close by, was the scene of a UFO incident as far back as 1958, when James Black of Balgreen Road observed a long silver-coloured object streaking across the evening sky above the hill.

It's significant to note that Edinburgh appears to be at the epicentre of a UFO triangle, which stretches from West Lothian across the city to East Lothian and up to Fife. In 1999, unexplained lights were seen over North Berwick Law. A search of the area revealed a strange piece of cloth hidden at the back of a run-down stone hut. This followed a report that a peculiar shard of metal had fallen from the sky and landed beside a walker on Traprain Law. Neither event proves that entities from outer space are visiting the area, and scientists who examined the cloth were dismissive of extraterrestrial origins though not everyone agrees with that verdict. But the odd lights reported were certainly in tune with similar sightings recorded over several decades by a variety of witnesses, and also tallied with the experience of abductees. Though it focused attention on alien encounters, the A70 abduction perhaps obscured several other cases where witnesses encountered beings who claim to have originated in distant worlds. On 16 February 1980, a man in his late thirties, living in Muirhouse, was woken by a disturbance. Going to the window he observed an object hovering between the block of flats where he lived and the adjacent building. It seems that either the UFO spotted him or had, for whatever reason, deliberately set out to attract his attention, for in the next moment he was struck by a beam of light. The light, coming from the UFO, froze his body and he found himself unable to move. At the same time he was aware of a strange smell which reminded him of sulphur. Immediately, he became aware of an entity which, he believed, spoke to him by telepathy. What it said is typical of the sort of message reported by those who claim to have encountered alien entities who then communicate with them, but with a twist. It warned John that the Earth was in danger, but that they would not allow the Earth to be harmed. They would take action to deal with those destroying it. The reason why they were interested in the planet's future came from the fact, they claimed, that they had once lived here. Having delivered the message they disappeared and John found that he could move again. But why they had appeared in this way and given such a message to an individual member of the public is hard to explain.

In the same year as the Muirhouse event, twenty-two-year-old Andrew Hennessey went through an abduction experience, taken from his home in the suburb of Portobello. As Andrew described it:

> In April 1980, in my bedroom, I was looking at the bookcase when I saw tiny green balls bouncing slowly over my books. I turned over in my bed and hoped they would go away. A while later, I looked back, but they were still there. I saw above the coffee table a hovering silver ball. It moved over to the foot of the bed and I heard a voice saying, 'Don't be afraid.'

When Andrew woke up the following day he found that he was so tightly tucked up in bed that he could not have done it himself. So what had happened? It was also 2 p.m., long past his usual waking time. So what had made him sleep on? He had vague memories of spending time with some grey-coloured aliens. It may seem a bit hazy, but these half-recalled recollections are typical of encounters of this kind, as Ed would testify.

Starting in August 1990, Ed went through several experiences with alien beings that he believed may have abducted him from his Morningside home. He described his experiences as 'memories,' but ones that clearly disturbed him. The incidents took place at the same time each morning, always between 12 a.m. and 3.30 a.m. On each occasion Ed felt both 'paralysed' and 'frightened.' Ed recalled lying on a bed of some kind surrounded by beings who appeared human-like, but with greyish coloured skin with a pinkish tinge. They were small, around five feet tall, and thin, with slow, lumbering movements. These beings wore clothes which looked as if they might be uniforms, an odd feature which is not often reported. But Ed could not recall any particular facial features so it is possible that the beings were wearing face coverings of some kind which obscured their heads. Ed did not know what to make of these events though he certainly found them unsettling.

As might be guessed, abduction experiences are rare events and often seem like isolated incidents, unrelated to wider UFO activity. Events around Gorebridge, however, run against this general trend. In the last few years, there have been many claimed sightings in the area, several caught on film. It has also been reported that there exists a system of underground tunnels around this location and that grey aliens dressed in uniforms have been observed at the entrance to the cavern network. These alleged sightings might fit with the ability of UFOs to disappear easily as, it has been suggested, they may have bases beneath the earth where they hide during the day. Unlikely though that may seem, many abductees have reported that rather than being lifted up into an orbiting UFO they believe that they were taken, in fact, underground. And Gary Wood, following his abduction on the A70, certainly had that suspicion.

Given the claims of the large amount of alien activity in the area, it may come as no surprise to learn that at least one abduction may have taken place. In 2007, the witness, a woman, was driving on a country road when her car engine and head-

lights abruptly cut out. She stepped out of the car and immediately became aware of a dark object hovering overhead with
a light shining from it. At that moment a car pulled up behind
her and a man came over, saying that his engine had suddenly
stopped working. He tried to phone for help, but found that
his mobile was 'dead.' Only then did he appear to catch sight
of the object above them. He seemed disturbed by what he was
seeing, but the UFO gradually moved away and as it did so
both car engines re-started. When the witness arrived at work,
as much as twenty minutes could not be accounted for. What
had happened during that missing time? Nobody can be sure.
This collection of incidents may be controversial, but it
undoubtedly fits a general pattern of UFO activity in, around
and over the capital, although there may be different interpretations over what was involved. However, there is a real interest across the UK about what is happening here, so much so
that, in June 2007, I was interviewed by Jeremy Paxman about
UFO activity in Scotland on the *Newsnight* programme, particularly about whether sightings of back triangular shaped objects
could, in fact, be secret military aircraft. It's certainly possible,
but could it really explain all UFO reports?

If alien beings are indeed passing through Edinburgh's air
space, are they also invading people's homes? And if so what
are they up to? One witness appears to have been through an
alien encounter of a very strange kind. In January 1989, Stuart
was staying on his own in a basement flat in the Newington
area. The first odd incident he experienced took place when
he heard strange noises coming from the wardrobe. There was
nothing obvious to explain it so he dismissed it. Was this a
prelude to later events? Stuart had by now moved to new
accommodation. One night he returned to his room in the early
hours after meeting some friends. As he lay down on the bed
a strange atmosphere seemed to envelop the room. He felt as

if a heavy presence was hanging over his body as he lay with his eyes closed. The room was in darkness and, in the dark, Stuart could hear the pounding of his heart and fear gripped him. He felt that he could not move properly although he was not paralysed. Summoning up all his strength Stuart threw himself out of bed and flicked on the light. Nothing. The room looked perfectly normal. He clambered back into bed and lay down. Classical music started to play. He could hear it, realising right away that something odd was happening as it was not the sort of music that appealed to him at that time in his life. 'What the hell is going on?' he muttered, opening his eyes to gaze at the ceiling.

By now the music had stopped and Stuart allowed his eyes to drift down from the ceiling. It was then that he saw it; a living vortex of energy like a swirling mass. He was fascinated yet repelled by the sight. What was it that forced Stuart to glance in the direction of the window? The curtains weren't fully drawn and in the gap between he could make out a large almond-shaped eye staring at him. The gaze was one of power, almost as if an invisible beam of energy was being directed at him. He was fascinated by the eye, but at the same time he was not able to hold its gaze. The energy emanating from it forced him to look away. Stuart, however, did not feel that the mysterious watcher was in any way threatening him. All the time that this was going on, Stuart could hear the sound of passing traffic on the road so knew that this was no strange dream. It was real and he was wide awake. Then, suddenly, a disembodied head of the being floated straight through the glass and into the bedroom where it hung suspended in mid-air. Stuart stared in sheer disbelief. It looked like an insect-shaped head with two large, dark eyes.

When Stuart examined the window the following morning he noticed some scratches on the window pane. He judged the distance from the ground to the spot where he had seen the eye and then head appear as around three feet, which suggested that whatever he had seen was well below the usual human height in stature. In fact, what he had seen reminded him of the alien entities encountered in various parts of the world; the small, large-headed greys who most certainly do not have a human-like appearance. But these events raise several questions. Are 'aliens' and 'UFOs' truly from other far-off planets in galaxies millions of light years away? Or are they beings who may exist in dimensions that border our own and can visit us at will? Whatever their origin, 'aliens' seem to be appearing in ever-increasing number, as do sightings of UFOs. Perhaps someday soon the purpose —if there is a purpose — of all this strange activity over Edinburgh, will be revealed to us. That is certainly what some abductees believe.

8

Weird Edinburgh

In the summer of 2001, on a bright afternoon, a couple, Tom and Ellen, were walking along a path above Salisbury Crags on Arthur's Seat when they experienced a strange encounter. As they strolled they suddenly became aware of two weird-looking figures about a hundred yards away. Both were unusually tall and thin, over seven feet in height with spindle-like arms and legs. They were dressed completely in black. But it was what they did next which led the couple to pause and stare. Suddenly they dropped in unison on all fours and appeared to be sniffing the grass as if looking for something. Tom recalled:

> For an instant I thought I'd wandered into a scene someone was creating for a horror film of some sort. It was just so unearthly. Then one of the pair pulled a small object from his pocket and pushed it firmly into the ground. They both stood up turned round and caught sight of us watching them.

Tom and Ellen immediately sensed that their presence was not welcome. In fact the atmosphere turned menacing. Tom said:

> If it hadn't been for the fact that our neighbour couldn't get out that day and we took his Alsatian for some exercise to help

out, I'm not sure what might have happened. The dog started barking and that seemed to disturb the pair so we took the chance to head off smartly. After a few seconds I glanced back, rather nervously I admit, and they had vanished. I couldn't see them anywhere. That unnerved me too so I was glad to get back to the car.

Of course, there might be an innocent explanation for this bizarre event. But against that is the fact that the description given by Tom and Ellen of the figures they saw hardly fits the bill of normal human beings. And the behaviour they witnessed appears decidedly odd. However, their experience does fit a pattern. Just one more strange, unexplained event, on a hill which has been a focus of strange activity across the centuries. Arthur's Seat has been the scene of many unsolved mysteries. One in particular has remained a puzzle for almost two hundred years.

In 1836, a strange find was made by schoolboys playing on its slopes. Beneath three pieces of upright slate they discovered a small space dug into the hillside, which had clearly been intended as a secret spot of some kind. What they then pulled out has been the subject of controversy ever since. At some time, exactly when still isn't clear, someone had placed inside the hole seventeen miniature coffins, which had been arranged neatly in three layers. There were eight on the first and second tiers, but only one on top, suggesting that it had probably been intended to add a few more. The coffins had been expertly made, carved out of wood, with perfectly fitting lids kept in place by brass pins, and from which shone elaborate metal plates, just like the real thing. Each coffin was no more than four inches long. When the coffins were opened the mystery deepened. Inside each box, which was lined with coloured cloth, rested a small figure, fully dressed, wearing funeral clothes with black boots. It was clear that someone had gone to a lot of effort to create a realistic funeral scene. But why? There have been several suggestions. Perhaps the most far-fetched is that the coffins were some kind of child's toy. It's true that they were tiny, as youngsters' toys tend to be, but who would give or make such a thing for a child? And why hide them in such a remote spot?

Furthermore, it was clear that the boxes had been entombed over a long period as the ones at the bottom of the pile were in a much poorer condition than the ones on top. Hiding away the coffins had clearly been a venture which had covered at least several years, if not decades. It had been a purposeful and secret exercise. So could it have been an act of witchcraft? Confessions extracted in the sixteenth century from accused witches include details of magic rituals by which an effigy was given the name of the person who was destined to die. Some object, even just a strand of the victim's hair, would be attached to the figure and it would then be burnt or destroyed in some way. As the effigy crumbled so the person it represented would fade and die. These figures were, however, normally made from wax and not wood. Nor would they be left for years like the Arthur's Seat coffins, as the whole point was their destruction not their preservation.

No, I would suggest a far more sinister interpretation. My investigation of Satanist and black magic beliefs has led me to the conclusion that, while the figures were indeed made to represent individuals, it was not intended that these people should die. What the creators were seeking was control of each person's soul. Practitioners of the dark side of ritual magic believe firmly that, by using the correct ceremonies, a man can gain possession of another's life essence. If that essence can then be attached to a figure made to represent that person, then the black magician believes that he has control over that man or woman. It is almost like a form of voodoo although it has no such name in Edinburgh. Having created his magic the Satanist would wish to preserve and conceal his figures which, incidentally, would have to be made from a living material such as wood. It does neatly explain what was found and why it was placed there. Of course there are those who will doubt that there was anything strange about these coffins, but that would be to ignore the beliefs of those, whether true or not, that ritual magic can overcome the forces of nature and have a direct effect on individual lives.

Certainly the idea that our lives might be subject to outside forces beyond our influence does concern some people. One of the strangest cases that I investigated was that in which a woman was convinced that she had become subject to a jinx. It seems a disturbing thing to believe, but a series of events occurred in a short space of time which suggested, in spite of scepticism, that something more than simple bad luck was at work. It appears to have started when Lucy rented a house on the north side of the town. Streams of invisible energy run across the city called ley lines and Lucy, who was keenly inter-ested in dowsing, was convinced that these were especially strong in the area around her home. She didn't realise at first that this energy might have a negative impact, and only became aware of it when her health rapidly went downhill. Doctors seemed unable to help and she was gradually being worn into the ground without being sure exactly why. Searching for answers, she turned to experienced dowsers for help and an attempt was made to divert the energy streams by putting down suitable stones, containing quartz, at particular locations. But, to Lucy's dismay, these efforts did not bring about any imme-diate improvement.

To Lucy these events, which some might have put down to simple bad luck, were part of a pattern. For years she had sensed that she was the victim of a jinx of some kind. The feeling gradually came over her, but was intensified by odd events she experienced. One day she was convinced that she had seen the word 'jinx' in a car number plate and that this had a special message meant for her. Another time, she came home to find that her front door had been broken down by the police. The story she was told was that there was concern about her health as she hadn't been seen by the neighbours for several days. Lucy found this hard to understand as, although she often spoke to her neighbours, days could pass by without seeing anyone. It was the second time that her door had been broken down for no clear reason and to Lucy it was inexplicable and part of the jinx. Immediately after this incident, Lucy's dog fell ill and was given only twenty-four hours to live. It eventually pulled through, but did not make a full recovery.

The jinx continued. Lucy was given a crystal to bring good luck and combat negativity. She put it in an envelope and left it on the sofa intending to find a safe place to keep it. She went into another room to type, but when she came back the crystal had vanished. It hadn't slipped down the side of the sofa and, according to Lucy, had simply disappeared into thin air. It seemed as if 'something' was determined to make Lucy's life as difficult as possible. There were many similar incidents, a lot more, she believed, than would be encountered in the normal run of life.

Lucy's experience raises a number of issues. Having dowsed her house when these events were going on I would confirm that there were strong energy streams running through all the rooms. It seems the case that such energy can affect individual health. Certainly the Chinese have believed so for thousands of years, but it's less clear why this should bring about a run of bad luck, so much so that a person might feel they were jinxed. Could the effect on health produce such a result, make one imagine that one's luck was worse than it is? Or are there elements in the universe which can play dice with our lives and, like rolling a series of ones when you want to roll a six, throw us a run of never ending bad luck?

Whatever the truth, my view, after years of using dowsing rods and discussion with fellow dowsers, is that energy can have a variety of effects and that nowhere is free of their influence. In 2004, when Heart of Midlothian were using Murrayfield to play home matches and there was talk of their moving there permanently, I offered to dowse both grounds to compare the effects that each would have on the ability of players to compete. I offered my services to the Hearts' board so that they and the supporters could judge the impact that moving to Murrayfield would have on the success of the team. As well as considering the financial position the board, I thought, should take into account the implication for the well-being of the Hearts' players in moving location. The *Evening News* covered my proposal under the heading: PARANORMAL EXPERT TO GET HEARTS ON RIGHT LINES.

My reasons for doing this were clear. An enclosed space like a football ground is criss-crossed by ley lines. You can get streams of negative and positive energy and an enclosed space is affected by the balance between these two forces. These streams of energy can have a physical effect on players, especially as they are taking part in intense activity. Teams are often successful at their home grounds because their bodies learn to attune to these streams of energy. Ideally, before any team considers moving ground, they should take into account the energy flow of the area they are moving to and the impact it may have. The Hearts' board did not take me up on the offer, but Hearts' legend Gary McKay was reported in the *Evening News* as saying that, 'Anything that's going to give the team an advantage in the long-term is fine by me.' Given the competitive nature of the football world, examining the impact of energy lines on your ground, whether it be Tynecastle or Easter Road, is surely worth consideration.

But could invisible tunnels of energy linking our world with who knows what or where explain a whole range of odd events, even the appearance of strange beasts? Phantom cats arouse much controversy. Are they pumas or some other large animal which has escaped from captivity? Or could they be alien creatures who have, by accident, entered the Earth from other dimensions? Or do they even exist? It seems hard to dispute that we are dealing with a genuine phenomenon. There have been too many close-up sightings to doubt it.

In the summer of 1979, a witness near the village of Roslin, where Rosslyn Chapel is located, glimpsed a large animal crossing a path nearby. He got a good view of the beast as, apparently, it was less than six feet from him. At such close range it is hard to believe that, when the witness states that what he saw was a puma, he could have made a mistake. The 'cat' was a golden colour like that of a typical Labrador with a black bar running across its face. The beast then leapt over a clump of ferns and raced uphill where it stopped for a moment and looked back allowing the witness another view. From this the witness was convinced that the animal was pregnant. If he was correct it would imply that there was at least one other puma roaming the countryside around Edinburgh.

An animal of a similar colour was seen three years later, in May 1982, by a woman out walking with her husband and children along a disused railway track near Penicuik. Mrs McKinnon described the creature as being around the size of a lion with gold-coloured fur and a long tail. The animal appeared to be preoccupied with prowling a small area of ground, which it did for several minutes while Mrs McKinnon kept it under observation. The beast gave no indication that it was aware of the family watching it from the path below.

This could not have been the same animal seen the following month, June 1982, apparently stalking sheep at a nearby farm, as this animal was described as being 'dark grey' in colour with a 'dark sheen' across its back. The beast was no smaller than twenty inches in height, with a long body, large ears and a tail measuring around three feet. It appeared to be preparing to attack animals in the field, though it seems it did not make a move at this time. Eventually the beast went away. Police were called and with the help of the SSPCA a search was made of the area, without success. However, a few days later, a monk at a nearby abbey reported seeing a similar animal with a dark body running across fields. Animal experts were convinced that a puma, or a large cat-like beast, was active as they were aware that a sheep had been killed in the area the previous weekend. This, apparently, had been in a manner which suggested that a large animal had been responsible.

The truth is that reports of an unidentified beast have been made by a considerable number of witnesses over the past few decades. The exact dates of some of these are unclear. However, they include a mother and daughter coming across a large puma-like cat sitting in the middle of the road as they drove towards West Linton. The beast stared at the car for a few seconds before jumping a gate and disappearing into the countryside. And a group of walkers glimpsed an animal they believed to be a puma, again in the Pentlands, as they followed the Nine Mile Burn route.

One puzzling aspect is that though incidents keep occurring there are significant time gaps, periods when the beasts simply seem to disappear. There appear to have been fewer sightings, for example, during the 1980s, but then the phantom beast returned in 1997, with a fresh rash of sightings. A puma-like creature was reported by a motorist after she saw it lying at the side of the road. She thought it might be unwell which chimed with a sighting by a second witness at a different location who thought the animal he saw might have an injured leg. Significantly though, there were no reports of sheep being attacked. As significant in my view is the comment from the SSPCA as reported by the Edinburgh *Evening News:* 'We've had reports of many sightings over the years, but we've never been able to confirm them. However, parts of West Lothian are quite desolate — there's no knowing what's up there.' The discovery, however, of large cat-like paw prints, following a report from a woman in Breich that she had seen a puma-like animal, maybe does suggest that we are dealing with a flesh-and-blood creature, though it remains surprisingly elusive.

This was certainly the view of some. In 1997, Brian Wood spent time searching the Bathgate Hills after several sightings of a black, puma-like animal which had been spotted padding through the streets of local towns and villages. Brian had an encounter of his own while walking his dog near Boghall in West Lothian, in April 1997. He heard the noise of leaves rustling and as he turned to look caught sight of a creature which resembled a panther. He described it as around four feet long and three feet in height. It leapt out from a mass of shrubbery then shot past him, before effortlessly jumping a fence at least six feet high.

Perhaps these phantom beasts have been around for a long time and that would explain a series of bizarre attacks on sheep on the west side of the Pentland Hills in the 1930s. However, on this occasion, no one even caught a glimpse of the creature which must have been responsible for the incidents. The idea that a 'big cat' was roaming the area would have been dismissed, at that time, as laughable. But the world has moved on and 'phantom cats' are certainly being taken more seriously, And if a puma was out there eighty years ago, it would certainly put paid to the explanation that irresponsible owners released such pets into the wild after the passing of the Dangerous Animals Act of 1975, which banned their ownership. These bizarre beasts have undoubtedly been around for much longer, and sightings of these creatures, their very appearance, seems to lie at the edge of reality. Attacks on sheep seem the most obvious sign of their presence, but do these incidents really fit the pattern of 'big cat' hunting methods? Not in every case.

In 1995, a sheep was killed in a bizarre manner, not far from Edinburgh airport. The farmer on whose land the sheep died claimed that it had been killed by a fox, but that was disputed by others. The cause of death appeared to be a massive wound around the throat, which looked as if it had been ripped open by powerful jaws. Such an attack seemed beyond the power of a fox, so might it have been the victim of another animal — the mysterious 'black cat?' It certainly seemed possible and fitted with sightings of such a creature. However, there were doubts. Why hadn't the puma removed the carcass, or at least consumed it, rather than just leaving it where it died? And investigators claimed that parts of the sheep had been carefully cored out, almost surgically, as if organs might have been removed deliberately, for preservation or use of some kind. So did the event fit more into those linked to 'alien mutilation', as reported from several parts of the USA? The jury is out as the evidence is conflicting, but the incident is undoubtedly a strange one.

If odd events are puzzling, the absence of phenomena can generate equal bemusement. In the 1980s and 1990s, hundreds of crop circles appeared across parts of south-west England. A variety of explanations was given for their arrival. To some they were an attempt by aliens to contact us, or the physical marks of a landed UFO. To others they were a sign from 'Mother Earth' herself, that she was angry at the way man was destroying the environment. Some scientists argued that they were

being produced by a hitherto little known physical phenomenon, but one which could be explained by rational, scientific
measurement. Two individuals claimed to have hoaxed the lot.
The full truth of what had happened is still being debated.

So why did crop circles seem to give Scotland a miss? In
total it appears that not even two dozen examples have been
seen here. I investigated several of them. A few were made close
to Edinburgh. One formed in a field by the side of Linlithgow
Loch. Another appeared on farmland near to Bonnybridge.
There were a couple of examples in East Lothian and the
Borders, another near Crieff and the furthest north was in
Corpach, close to Fort William. The largest I saw, however,
consisting of three concentric rings, was near Limekilns, in
Fife. Whilst the formations that appeared in counties like
Wiltshire became ever more complex, all the ones in Scotland
were little more than a simple circle of flattened crop, or rough
grass. The one that formed closest to Edinburgh was beside
the airport and was drawn to my attention by a passenger on
an inbound flight, though not till several days had passed.
Again, it was of a basic circular formation but, unfortunately,
the crop was cut down before I had the chance to take any
measurements.

The absence of the phenomenon from an area like Edinburgh,
with extensive crop-growing land roundabout, is puzzling.
Given the volume of UFO sightings you might expect, if there
was some connection, that circles would be formed. So why
weren't they? Is there a clue in a similar type of incident? One
which appeared in the heart of the city?

Crop circles on your lawn? This phenomenon, rarely reported,
was seen and documented by John Morrison. He wrote:

While on a visit to some relatives in Edinburgh on Friday, 13
September 1996, I was told about some unusual circles that

had appeared in their garden only days before. The owner, Andrew, had been mowing the lawn several days before my arrival and as he finished the job he noticed several rings on the lawn. The rings seemed to be due to the death of some of the grass as it was yellow/discoloured. He felt that this was very strange as they do not use any type of pesticide or weed killers in their garden. I checked around the garden to see if any tools could have caused the rings but could find nothing capable of creating them. I checked the plant pots around the garden, but they were all too small in diameter to have caused damage to the grass. Only one ring was very well defined all the way round, the others being three-quarters and faintly defined. An unusual feature of the rings was that they were easier to see from a height of about four metres than at ground level.

The immediate issue that springs to mind was whether some object of some kind had landed in Andrew's garden. According to John's measurements and the diagram that he drew, the rings formed a triangle with an uppermost one pointing roughly north and the base of the triangle formed by the other two rings, with one slightly higher than the other. The rings were not large. The topmost was 36.5 centimetres across and the two forming the 'base' were 36 centimetres and the third of a similar dimension. An added curiosity was that two rings of the same appearance and size had formed slightly to the right of the top circle. It did look as if an object had pressed hard into the lawn and, as it did so, it destroyed the surface. The appearance of these circles was reminiscent of those that had appeared in farmers' fields. The principal difference, apart from size, was that the area within the circles had been damaged rather than simply flattened. This event then, I would suggest, was more in keeping with accounts that described small UFO-type objects, maybe remotely controlled, landing in people's gardens, of which there were several reports from around the world. In this instance, no object was seen, but there were certainly many sightings around this time of UFOs across the Edinburgh skies. So does this explain the city's only 'crop' circle? It's a mystery, but an intriguing one.

At one time, these small circles might have been laid at the door of quite a different being; the 'nature spirits' or 'fairies'. When we think of fairies we have an idea of a small winged creature, delicate and cute. That, however, was not how fairies were traditionally seen in Scotland. They were viewed as a race of people similar to humans, who lived in a netherworld beneath the ground. They possessed fantastic powers including that of invisibility. They often entered people's homes unannounced, kidnapped the unwary and would generally make a nuisance of themselves, especially if you upset them.

There's no doubt that Edinburgh has a long tradition of fairy sightings stretching back over several hundred years. In the seventeenth century, Calton Hill was reputed to be a site beneath which could be found a fairy mound. George Burton, who visited Edinburgh in the 1660s, claimed to have spoken to a youth who told him that, every Thursday night, he went inside Calton Hill which he entered by a set of invisible gates. He told Burton that underneath the hill was a suite of rooms in which the fairy folk lived. The lad also claimed to have psychic powers and predicted events yet to be. Burton tried to follow the youth into the hill, but was given the slip. Whilst the account might appear far-fetched it has to be said that it is in keeping with many similar reports from across Scotland at this time. And Calton Hill was only one site where it was said fairies had set up home. Arthur's Seat contains several such places still known as a 'fairy knowe' and where that appears on a map you will know that the location was, at one time, seen as a habitation of the fairy people. Times have changed, but fairies have certainly not abandoned the capital. Far from it. In the 1850s, Hugh Miller claimed to have seen fairies in his garden in Portobello. In 1958, Mrs Van Horne reported that a gnome was inhabiting her house in Rothesay Place. He was about a foot tall dressed in red trousers with a brown jacket. Although invisible to most visitors as he sat on the mantelpiece or sideboard, some claimed that they had indeed glimpsed the diminutive being. Mrs Van Horne reported that he had been following her around for years.

But the most extensive sightings of 'nature spirits' was made by the mystic R. O. Crombie. Crombie claimed that, while sitting in the Botanic Gardens one sunny afternoon in March 1966, he suddenly became aware of a three foot high figure dancing around a nearby tree. He did a double take as what he saw was something extraordinary. The 'boy', as he described him, had 'shaggy legs and cloven hooves' and also a 'pointed chin' and 'ears.' However, perhaps, strangest of all was the two horns projecting from his forehead. The creature's legs were covered in fine hair and his skin was light brown. Crombie overcame his shock and called out to the entity.

The creature was startled and surprised that Crombie could see him, suggesting either that he believed himself normally invisible or that he inhabited some kind of parallel world in which humans did not normally interact. Events now turned even more weird. The creature got into conversation with Crombie and told him that his name was Kurmos. He agreed to go home with Crombie and the pair walked though the garden gates and along Arboretum Road. Kurmos was invisible to all but Crombie. Back in his flat Crombie and Kurmos talked some more until Kurmos told him it was time for him to return to the Gardens. Crombie opened the door to let him out and Kurmos ran down the steps, his form fading away as he reached the last one.

*The Botanic Gardens, Inverleith – more than just an
attractive haunt for plant lovers. It is here that the mystic
R. O. Crombie encountered and conversed with strange
creatures from another dimension.*

One might be forgiven for believing that somehow Crombie
had experienced a strange waking dream if it wasn't for the
fact that this incident was simply the start of a series of bizarre
encounters. Crombie returned to the Botanic Gardens on
several subsequent occasions during March and April, and
each time, when he called out Kurmos's name, the faun
appeared.

At the end of April events became a little more disturbing.
Crombie had been visiting a friend's house near the Meadows.
His journey back home took him along Meadow Walk, over
George IV Bridge and down the Mound. Princes Street lay
before him. As he reached the National Gallery he felt a strange

atmosphere descend on him which made him feel as if he was walking though water. A warm sensation enveloped him and his body tingled. He sensed that 'something' was about to happen though he could hardly have expected what appeared. It was a being who told him, 'I am the Devil,' and added that if he didn't believe him to look at his cloven hooves, shaggy legs and the horns on his head. Crombie later wrote that he had 'a musk-like' animal smell.

Incredibly, Crombie later denied that he was at all afraid, even when the creature put his arm around him. He did not believe that this entity was the 'Devil', but Pan, the god of nature, as written of by the ancient Greeks. The entity, what-ever it was, walked with Crombie across Princes Street into George Street. Crombie had managed to convince himself that he was not meeting any evil spirit and told the 'Devil' that he believed he was, in reality, Pan. As if by magic, and rather too conveniently, the entity produced a set of pipes and played what Crombie described as a 'strange tune', which he could not later remember. As they came to Crombie's house the entity disappeared. Crombie saw him again on two occasions outside the city. At these the 'Devil' appeared surrounded by various entities, including elves, gnomes, and fairies.

So was Crombie experiencing an expedition into another world or, as some have argued, deluding himself? Crombie never doubted that these events were rooted in reality. To him they were as much a part of the real world as taking a bus ride and his visions had a very practical effect. One of the reasons why the world-famous Findhorn Foundation chose its location in the north of Scotland was down to Crombie's claim that the nature spirits had appeared to him and told him that this was a suitable spot for their enterprise. Crombie was a founder of this influential community, created for those who sought a more spiritual type of life. He certainly believed that happiness could be earned through working with his friends among the nature spirits.

Some believed that, in fact, Crombie had drifted into another dimension; a kind of 'out of the body' experience or 'OBE'. Since the 1960s, the world has became more aware of OBEs and they are now a widely reported phenomenon. It's interesting to note, however, that as far back as the 1930s instances were being documented in the city. In May 1933, the *Evening Dispatch* reported the case of a woman from Newington who, 'when she was very ill had the unusual sensation of feeling that she was outside of her body, of standing looking down on it as it lay on the bed.' She explained that she saw 'her sister standing with the doctor looking down on her body.' She heard him say that he would give her an injection, following which he indicated that they had better leave the room for a short time 'as the patient must be kept very quiet.'

There is an aspect to this incident which we don't usually find in OBE cases as the woman added, 'they left the room and I went with them.' She had left 'her body behind on the bed, and she listened to what they said in the next room.' This suggests that the incident lasted for several minutes and that is not typical of events of this nature. Unfortunately, there is no indication of when the experience ended or whether the woman involved attempted to confirm with her sister and the doctor if, what she heard, was what they had actually said. In fact most OBE cases are connected with near-death experiences and, though the lady in Newington was unwell, she was by no means in a critical state. Her experience, however, suggests that the spirit can leave the body and, when it does, still has the ability to think and understand. All of which may have played a part in R. O. Crombie's encounters. But if the soul is a separate part of us and can leave the body does that explain reincarnation?

The belief in reincarnation, the idea that each of us is born again and again, is usually linked to the mystic religions of the Far East, and both Hinduism and Buddhism immediately spring to mind. But, in fact, the view that we return many times to Earth to live new lives has a long tradition in Scotland with Edinburgh, as befits a capital city, playing a leading role. It was a key part of the Druid religion, the pagan sect which influenced many pre-Christian beliefs and whose views are still held by some today. In fact, reincarnation has re-emerged in recent years with many Edinburgh citizens claiming that they have 'lived before.' You can even join reunion groups in the city where members discuss each others' past lives, not necessarily lived on this world. Edinburgh mystic Ray Tod was convinced that he had lived before as an Egyptian priest and could list the names of those he had met during his previous years on Earth. He had a vivid memory of his life in Ancient Egypt. Incidentally, the reincarnated soul can return as either a man or woman and Theresa, a shop assistant, told me of her time as a Roman Soldier, and of having been speared and killed on a battlefield.

But being reborn may not be a straightforward task as Thomas explained.

I remember making a particular decision to choose this life. I was given a choice of fourteen or fifteen types of life in Western Europe. I was shown the potential for development in each family, of the way in which I would develop in each different set of circumstances. I remember lying in my cot at the age of two looking at a lake scene and the water started shaking. My spirit guide appeared and asked me if I was sure I wanted to do it this way. I was having very involved conversations at the age of two! Just before I chose my life I remember that I was drinking from a cup. However, I can't actually remember being born.

Thomas, however, chose a life in twentieth-century Edinburgh on that occasion.

Memories of past lives seem, for most people, to be hidden and only emerge under certain circumstances. In 2004, a Swedish man, Jesper Bood, claimed that he had lived a previous life as a boy in the East Lothian town of Dunbar in the 1850s. Mr Bood had been regressed hypnotically for a programme about reincarnation, made by the Swedish company Strix Television AB. Recalling memories under hypnosis, Mr Bood, who had never visited Scotland, remembered that he had been born as John Smith in Dunbar in 1852. His father had been a blacksmith, also called John, and his mother's name was Mary Craig. He himself later became a fisherman, marrying a local woman called Betsy.

Astonishingly, investigation of these claims turned up facts which appeared to show that these memories were by no means fanciful. The name he had given for his parents did exist and the records revealed that a thirty-year-old John Smith had married a woman called Elizabeth which often, in those days, became 'Betsy'. The family's home was in a location known as Gateside where a forge did once exist, which fitted with the memory of a father who had been a blacksmith. Mr Bood recalled a wealth of detail, talking of a thirty-minute walk to school and giving a description of Dunbar Parish Church. He said that the church, which he could see from the school window, sat close to the sea, as it does. Local experts were also able to recognise Woodburn School, demolished in the 1950s, from Mr Bood's account, and the fisherman's tavern, still standing, which he said he had visited on many occasions in this past life.

However, the most detailed case, which many believe provides powerful evidence in support of reincarnation, is that of Ada Kay. Ada was born in Lancashire in the 1920s, but the events that were to trigger a life-long obsession with Edinburgh did not start till she was eighteen years old, when she joined the ATS and was posted to the capital to be stationed eventually near Fairmilehead. Crossing the Scottish border she was swept by a wave of patriotism and experienced the sensation that she was at last 'coming home.' This feeling had a more profound implication than she could maybe have guessed at the time. Visiting the ancient regalia of the Scottish crown in Edinburgh Castle, she had a vision of bright red blood trickling down the royal sword as it rested in its display case. Further visions followed during the succeeding days. She kept seeing Edinburgh as it had been hundreds of years ago in the sixteenth century. In these visions the streets and buildings of modern Edinburgh vanished and in their place were forests, lochs, hunting grounds, wild beasts and acres of free land. Ada started walking obsessively up and down the Royal Mile, fascinated by the medieval aspects of the 'Old Town'. She sensed that it had a deeper meaning for her, but what could that be?

One evening passing through the Lawnmarket, Ada spotted an open door dimly lit by candlelight. Something in her head told her that she was expected to go in as there were people waiting to meet her. Just then a man appeared who bowed to her and ushered her inside. At that instant everything disappeared and Ada found herself standing in the street. When she tried to locate the door the next day it was simply nowhere to be found, but the visions continued. This time she 'saw' lines of old-fashioned ships cruising up and down the Forth. Ada was now convinced that she was experiencing visions of past events without understanding why it was happening. Having decided to quit the army she took the train down south, but as she crossed the border she had another strange experience. As she sat in the railway carriage, Ada saw a reflection of herself in the window, but it was not really her. It was the image of someone with a very different, masculine face. Above his head Ada could see a circle of gold, studded with blue stones which sparkled in a halo of light.

Several years passed before Ada manged to make sense of it all; time during which she became a successful playwright and a BBC script writer. In 1959 she returned to Edinburgh and set out to learn more about Scotland's history. She was stunned on seeing a portrait of James IV to realise that he was the person she had seen in the reflection of the train window. He also had red hair just as she did. Ada became aware that thinking of the Battle of Flodden, at which James had been killed in September 1513, sent shivers coursing through her body. She sensed her identification with King James growing ever more intense and, in 1966, wrote a play about his life, which seemed to flow easily from what she now believed to be genuine memories of having been James in a past life. In August 1967, while visiting Jedburgh, Ada, or A. J. Stewart as she was now known following her marriage, experienced a traumatic memory of 'her' death at the Battle of Flodden. She saw clearly the swords as they cut into her body and snatched her life away. To Ada this horrific experience was the final proof that the death she had suffered was real and that everything she had experienced only made sense if reincarnation was a fact. In 1970, she published *Falcon. The Autobiography of His Grace James the fourth of Scotland,* described as 'Presented by A. J. Stewart'. It was an account of her former life as the king. This was followed, in 1978, by *Died 1513 – Born 1929* the autobiography of A. J. Stewart. There will be those, of course, who will wonder if it was all in Ada Kay's imagination. But Ada, or A. J. Stewart, was an intelligent woman who considered carefully the incidents she had been through and, only after long consideration, did she decide that for her there could be no other explanation. At one time she had been King James IV, reborn in the twentieth century as Ada Kay.

Ada Kay did not claim it, but there's maybe another strange phenomenon that reincarnation explains; that of premonition. A 'premonition' a warning that something awful is going to happen has been frequently reported. One incident was recorded as far back as July 1860, when a woman in Portobello was warned by a spirit voice that her daughter, Emma, was going to be involved in an accident. The woman herself related the story:

> I had told my Emma that I would let her go out to play from three till four and as she was alone I suggested that she go to the 'railway garden', a strip of land between the sea and the railway. A few minutes after she left, I distinctly heard a voice saying to me, 'Send for her at once or something terrible will happen.' I ignored it, but a few minutes later the same voice began to say the same words to me, but more forcibly. I still resisted and used all my imagination to divine what could happen to the child. I thought about an encounter with a mad dog, but dismissed it as absurd, although I was now beginning to feel anxious. I still resisted doing anything, but soon the voice repeated the warning. 'Send for her immediately or something terrible will happen.' At the same time I was gripped with violent trembling and extreme terror. I got up quickly, rang the bell and told the servant to go for my daughter, repeating the voices' words, 'or something terrible will happen'.

The servant went out and found her daughter. Shortly after, a train went off the railway line, crashing into the wall and then the strip of land where the daughter used to play. Three men were killed outright and several injured. There's no doubt that had little Emma not been brought home she would have been among the dead as the engine had hit the very area of rock that she liked to sit on. So had the woman been reliving an episode of life that she had been through before? Could it have been a 'guardian angel' calling from the spirit domain? In the world of the supernatural nothing is ever clear-cut.

There's another strange tale about premonitions with a decidedly odd twist, which was recorded in the summer of 1844. William, whose father owned a large house in Edinburgh, was a twelve year old who the family believed had the power of 'second sight.' He reported having 'visions' some of which appeared to be very distressing. One evening, according to the report of the time, 'when the family was all together they had suddenly seen William turn pale and become motionless.' At the same time, they heard a voice, which appeared to come from William himself, saying, 'I see a child asleep lying in a velvet box with a sheet of white satin and wreaths and flowers all around. Why are my parents weeping?' William's parents were understandably shocked and woke William who, coming to his senses, treated the whole episode as a bit of a joke and ran off to play. A week later the family was sitting outside having had lunch. They noticed that William was not with them and, being unable to find him, a full search of the grounds of the house was set in motion. Eventually, William was found in a small loch. He had, it seemed, been trying to get into a boat moored there, slipped, fallen into the water and drowned. It appears that, bizarrely, twelve-year-old William had predicted his own death correctly.

William, unfortunately, never had the chance to grow up, never had the opportunity, as a man of his background might, to join the clubs which were such a part of Edinburgh life during this era, although even by the time of the lad's death these societies were becoming more cautious about their behaviour. That hadn't always been the case.

Some two hundred years ago, Edinburgh was witness to a bizarre phenomenon; the growth of several private clubs whose members engaged in weird practices and rites. They adopted strange names including the 'Sulphur Club', the 'Horn Club' and the 'Demi-reps'. Membership was exclusive and only select people were allowed to join, but what they lacked in numbers they made up for in the scandal they created. It was rumoured that, at their weekly meetings, they mocked the Bible and Christian beliefs, preferring strange ceremonies they had devised themselves. More scurrilous were claims that, though women were not officially permitted to join, some were allowed in so that members could take part in group sex and other orgiastic rites. We know from investigation of the 'Beggar Bennison' club, which originated in St Andrews but claimed support from Edinburgh, that its members wore ceremonial robes and worshipped a bizarre historical relic, a wig made from the pubic hair of Charles II's mistresses. Even stranger was their practice of measuring the length of each others' penises on a special plate while a woman, her face covered by a cloth, lounged naked in a broad armchair. But what, above all, concerned some was that leading men of the city were said to be involved, including judges, MPs and town councillors. It seemed as if the degrading activities engaged in by these clubs could corrupt the whole city.

With hindsight it appears that people were getting worked up over very little. The clubs have long gone and maybe their influence on Edinburgh society was exaggerated. And one might be inclined to think that if it hadn't been for events involving the infamous Hell Fire Club whose reputation for debauchery sparked a succession of shock waves which reverbate to the present day. Its activities were considered so bizarre that it was seen as outrageous in a very lax period of history as far as morals were concerned. It also had some of the most influential people in the land as its members. The club was probably founded in London by Sir Francis Dasherwood, in the 1760s, and the exact link between the London and Edinburgh branches is not clear. But in terms of activity they were certainly on the same wavelength. Down south the Hell Fire Club engaged in every kind of perverse activity including incest. Sexual orgies were held, with 'temples' set up secretly inside churches to carry out late-night weird religious rites. Naked women were laid out on altars on which inverted crosses were placed, while 'priests' carried out the club's secret ritual. Hell Fire members were fascinated by fire and may well have practised the ancient rite of fire worship. Indeed, it was claimed that several fires in Edinburgh were started by the club as part of their ritual activities. This certainly happened in England, where Hell Fire members were prosecuted for fire-raising, and in Glasgow, where the club burned down the Tron Kirk. However, no one in Edinburgh, despite suspicion, was charged and some believed that that was down to powerful friends among the judiciary.

And that may well be true for, in spite of the bizarre activities of the club, it boasted many prominent individuals among its members. They included several well-known Scots, even the Earl of Bute who became Prime Minister in 1762, the first Scot to hold the office after the Act of Union. He appointed the Hell Fire Club founder, Francis Dasherwood, as his Chancellor of the Exchequer. Oddly, though the names of those who were active in the Edinburgh Hell Fire Club are largely unknown, as is the case in Glasgow. Arranging a 'cover-up' has long been an option for those in authority and is by no means an invention of the twenty-first century.

But perhaps the most bizarre club of all did not appear till the last years of the nineteenth century. The Hermetic Order of the Golden Dawn was set up in the 1890s and included among its members the notorious Satanist Aleister Crowley, dubbed the 'Great Beast', a practitioner of black magic who, since his death in 1947, has become an iconic figure for followers of the 'dark side' of witchcraft. On the other hand, the poet William Butler Yeats also joined and, as is often the case in magical orders, it included both the innocent and determinedly evil. The Edinburgh branch of the order was set up by the mystic John Brodie-Innes, who established the Amen-Ra temple. Innes and his fellow members took ritual magic seriously and when a dispute broke out between the Edinburgh and London branches of the Golden Dawn the air was electric with psychic battles fought in the ether, and magic spells cast to do down the opposition. Crowley, however, proved too strong and Innes abandoned the Amen-Ra temple though he set up other magic groups, which continued into the 1920s. There are still followers of the magic rites he created active in Edinburgh today, though they prefer to work away from the limelight. According to these adepts, they were responsible for a historic event — it was their magic which brought about the return of the mystical 'Stone of Scone' to Scotland.

Within the ancient walls of Edinburgh Castle you can visit one of the nation's most treasured possessions. The famous Stone of Destiny, the 'throne' on which centuries of Scottish kings were crowned, was returned to the capital in 1997, after it had been held in London for several hundred years. There is a long tradition that the Stone of Destiny was the same rock which, in Biblical legend, Jacob used one night as a pillow. As he slept he dreamt of a ladder which reached from Earth to Heaven, and he heard God's voice calling him. In modern times, this tradition has been interpreted in different ways. To some Jacob was in touch with beings from another world. To others he was making contact with spirit entities. But it is widely agreed that the rock must have acted as a mystical key of some kind.

Legend has it that the Stone of Destiny came to Scotland by way of Egypt and Ireland. It has a reputation as an object possessing great paranormal powers. Some say it still has, and point to the fact that within three years of the stone's return to Scotland a parliament, the first for three hundred years, was set up. In fact, the parliament's first meeting was held a short distance from where the Stone now sits. When Edward I took the Stone away with him in 1296, did he somehow weaken the soul of Scotland? Did that soul return with the arrival of the Stone in Edinburgh, or was it simply coincidence? Of course, you'd have to believe that such a thing as a country has a soul. And maybe the whole idea appears far-fetched, but, like so many events involving the paranormal, it has to be admitted that it was a very curious coincidence indeed.

So why is Edinburgh a city of such weird and wonderful events? One thing that can surely be agreed is that the catalogue of strange incidents recounted in *Edinburgh After Dark* cannot be simply put down to over-active imaginations or collective hallucination. The variety of events experienced undoubtedly show that whatever the cause, 'something odd' is connected to the land on which the city stands. Those who wish to disbelieve will, of course, never be convinced till a ghost is 'captured' in a science laboratory or an alien being appears in Princes Street gardens. However, those with an open mind should at the very least have been given food for thought. Is the world truly limited to the everyday reality we experience as we go about our lives? Or are there beings, friendly and not so friendly, inhabiting unknown dimensions who from time to time enter by choice or design the world we call our own? The evidence suggests that whatever sceptics may think, we are truly not alone. It may be the case that Edinburgh is located in an area which acts as a window into other worlds and the city has become a playground of the bizarre as a result. Whatever the truth it seems that the capital and the supernatural have been, and will continue to be, closely and inescapably entwined.

Bibliography

Beaumont, William Comyns: *Britain: The Key to World History*. (Rider &Co, 1949).

Chambers, Robert: *Traditions of Edinburgh*. (W. & R. Chambers, 1868).

Coventry, Martin: *Haunted Places of Scotland*. (Goblinshead, 1999).

Evans, Lorraine: *Kingdom of the Ark*. (Simon & Schuster, 2001).

Grant, James: *Old and New Edinburgh*. (Cassells (3 Vols), 1882).

Halliday, Ron: *The A-Z of Paranormal Scotland*. (Black & White Publishing, 2000).

Halliday, Ron: *Evil Scotland*. (Fort, 2003).

Halliday, Ron: *McX: Scotland's X-Files*. (Black & White Publishing, 1987).

Halliday, Ron: *UFO Scotland*. (Black & White Publishing, 1998).

Harrison, John: *The History of the Palace of Holyrood*. (Blackwood, 1919).

Henderson, Jan-Andrew: *The Ghost that Haunted Itself*. (Mainstream, 2001).

Miles, David: *The Tribes of Britain*. (Weidenfeld & Nicolson, 2005).

Russo, Arlene: *Vampire Nation*. (John Blake, 2005).

Stewart, A. J.: *Died 1513 – Born 1929: the Autobiography of A. J. Stewart*. (Macmillan, 1978).

Wilson, A., Brogan, D., McGrail F.: *Ghostly Tales of Old Edinburgh*. (Mainstream, 1994).